The Spirit-Driven Church

Finding a church that is united, growing, and impacting lives for eternity is not impossible. But finding a church that has internal tension, unhappy people, and divided loyalties is all too common. Everyone wants to be a part of the former; no one wants to be a part of the latter.... How can we perpetuate the former? Robnett and Quist are on to something. It is not merely novel, but it is remarkably profound. Their solution is poignantly biblical, theologically consistent, and spiritually convincing. All of us in ministry should not only read this volume, but should put it into practice. Then the church that everyone desires to call home will be realized.

DR. BRUCE FONG
PRESIDENT, MICHIGAN THEOLOGICAL SEMINARY

I believe if church leaders and members would embrace the principles discussed in this book, there would be an explosive growth and expansion of the kingdom of God beyond anything we could imagine.

RICK BATTERSHELL, CPA

I want to applaud the authors for stepping in to fill a gaping hole in leadership books for the church. There are numerous Christian leadership books on the market. But there are very few that genuinely seek to start with deep dependence on God and move all the way to practical implementation without somehow transitioning to a ... "self-dependent" use of management principles. Tim and Allen do a remarkable job. Use this book, but keep your dependence on God!

PAUL RHOADS
EXECUTIVE VICE PRESIDENT, CHURCH RESOURCE MINISTRIES

It is unusual to read a book on leadership that so commands your attention. The authors adroitly weave real stories and experiences into exhortations to look to godly, Spirit-filled leaders who will enable churches to be transforming forces in the world. This fresh view of leadership and management emphasizes the work of God in forming the character of the leader. It is not just a book on "how to do leadership" but a "how to be a Spirit-filled leader." A must-read for church leaders and administrators.

DR. DONALD L. BRAKE
DEAN OF MULTNOMAH BIBLICAL SEMINARY, PORTLAND, OREGON

What stands out in this book is Timothy and Allen's passion and desire for the church to be truly God's church. Their call is for a genuine self-assessment of what we unintentionally and unfortunately have allowed many of our churches to become: ineffectual organizations operating on our own power and focused on our own agendas. A timely call for the church to listen to the heart of the Master.

RANDY POON
DIRECTOR GENERAL, STRATEGIC POLICY AND MANAGEMENT DEPARTMENT OF CANADIAN HERITAGE, OTTAWA, ONTARIO

This book is a fresh expression of how genuine, biblical servant leadership will enhance the twenty-first-century church. The authors' emphasis on Spirit-led leaders who allow God to form the culture of their churches will foster renewal and transformation of ministries. It is fantastic to see in print what I have heard these men talk about, experience, and teach in classrooms and seminars. All church leaders will be able to enrich their ministries with the wisdom in this book.

DR. LARRY AYERS
FORMER PRESIDENT, WESTERN SEMINARY; ADJUNCT PROFESSOR OF LEADERSHIP AND MANAGEMENT, MULTNOMAH BIBLICAL SEMINARY, PORTLAND, OREGON

Someone told me once that the Christian walk can be boiled down to two movements of the heart: a radical willingness to really hear God and the necessary radical willingness to obey—no matter what. This is the Spirit-driven church. Far too often we, the evangelical church, do homage to our own skills and efforts at the expense of really listening to God's Spirit. Dr. Tim Robnett and Allen Quist's new book, The Spirit-Driven Church, *will guide you into that willingness to listen to and obey the Holy Spirit's call.*

THE REVEREND BILL SENYARD
SENIOR PASTOR, PEACE VALLEY COMMUNITY CHURCH, CHALFONT, PENNSYLVANIA

The Spirit-Driven Church *brings focus to the key question for each church and its leaders: Are we doing what God is telling us to do in the way that God is telling us to do it? Tim Robnett and Allen Quist provide balanced, biblical, and practical insight for finding and then implementing the answer to that question. The principles in this book will transform the life and ministry of any church that puts them into practice.*

TROY ANDERSON
GENERAL COUNSEL, THE CITY CHURCH, SEATTLE, WASHINGTON

I loved the real-life analogies that are woven into the book! These are a means to uncovering blind spots that professionals and church leaders need to discover in order to follow the leading of the Spirit. I recommend this book to any church leader and, in particular, to anyone considering church leadership.

DENNIS A. LONG
PRESIDENT AND CEO, PACIFIC FINANCIAL CORPORATION

THE *Spirit* DRIVEN CHURCH

DR. TIMOTHY ROBNETT
& ALLEN H. QUIST

Victor®

The Bible Teacher's Teacher

COOK COMMUNICATIONS MINISTRIES
Colorado Springs, Colorado • Paris, Ontario
KINGSWAY COMMUNICATIONS LTD
Eastbourne, England

Victor® is an imprint of
Cook Communications Ministries, Colorado Springs, CO 80918
Cook Communications, Paris, Ontario
Kingsway Communications, Eastbourne, England

THE SPIRIT-DRIVEN CHURCH
© 2006 by Timothy Robnett and Allen H. Quist

Cover Design: Marks & Whetstone
Cover Photo: © BigStock Photo

The Web addresses (URLs) recommended throughout this book are solely offered as a resource to the reader. The citation of these Web sites does not in any way imply an endorsement on the part of the author or the publisher, nor does the author or publisher vouch for their content for the life of this book.

Published in association with the literary agency of Sanford Communications, Inc., 6406 NE Pacific St., Portland, OR 97213.

First Printing, 2006
Printed in the United States of America

1 2 3 4 5 6 7 8 9 10 Printing/Year 10 09 08 07 06

Unless otherwise noted, Scripture quotations are taken from the *Holy Bible, New International Version*®. *NIV*®. Copyright © 1973, 1978, 1984 by International Bible Society. Used by permission of Zondervan. All rights reserved. Scripture quotations marked NASB are taken from the *New American Standard Bible*, © Copyright 1960, 1995 by The Lockman Foundation. Used by permission; and NLT are taken from the *Holy Bible, New Living Translation*, copyright © 1996. Used by permission of Tyndale House Publishers, Inc., Wheaton, Illinois 60189. All rights reserved. Italics in Scripture have been added by the authors for emphasis.

ISBN-13: 978-0-7814-4373-9
ISBN-10: 0-7814-4373-3

LCCN: 2006925155

CONTENTS

FOREWORD

There is nothing more exciting than participating in a thriving, growing congregation that is obviously moved by God. I believe most Christians would give anything to be part of a church that is being radically renewed.

If we really want to see our churches become driven by the Holy Spirit, and if we want to see God radically transform his church across this country, we first must say "yes!" to the Holy Spirit's work in our own lives. Otherwise, how can we promote what we ourselves haven't experienced? How can we present what we don't know and have?

Wherever I've seen church renewal and revival, I've always traced it back to a small group of Christians who were broken over their sin, confessed it, were cleansed, and began a fresh walk with the indwelling Christ. It has to start somewhere. Why not ask God to let it start with you?

Have you ever dreamed about what God wants to do—starting with you—in your church, in your city? I believe God wants to use you.

If God renews you, you'll grow to love your church and pray for its people. And you'll pray for the church around the world. You won't have a sectarian bone in your body. Or if you do, you'll crucify it. Because if we're being led by the Holy Spirit, we will be diligent to do whatever God commands. And one of the primary commands, repeated eight times for us in the New Testament, is to "love one another." That applies to all Christians, whether or not we agree on every point of doctrine and practice.

When I was younger, I preached certain minor points of doctrine with conviction. Now I'm embarrassed because after further prayer and study I've changed my mind about a few of those details. What I'd learned earlier sounded good, but wasn't based squarely on a balanced view of God and his Word. So I've grown. That's good. Let's leave room for others to grow too.

Let's strive for the unity of the body of Christ—the church. Let's love our brothers and sisters in Christ, pray for them, and respect them as his Word commands. We won't see eye to eye on everything. But we can have unity because we were bought by the blood of the Savior, we're filled with his Spirit, and we're preaching his Word. That's our common ground, our basis for unity with all who are called by his name.

The biblical principles presented in this book are deep, yet simple. They're deep enough to challenge us for a lifetime, yet simple enough for most people to understand and apply immediately.

My prayer is that God will use this book to bless the whole church, here in this country and around the world. May he renew us all and give us boldness to allow our churches to be driven by his Holy Spirit.

Will you join me toward that end?

Luis Palau

ACKNOWLEDGMENTS

Words cannot express our deepest thanks to our Lord and Savior Jesus Christ for his creation, for our adoption into the family of God, for the ongoing work of the Holy Spirit in our lives, and for allowing us to minister to you through this book.

Everyone needs to know how much we love and appreciate our families: Tim's wife, Sharon, and their two adult children: their son, Joel and his wife, Kate, and their daughter, Karen.

Allen's wife, Mary, and their three adult children: son Andrew, son Daniel and his wife, Nellie, and their children, Emily and Matthew, and daughter, Naomi, and her husband, Brian, and their daughter, Nicole.

The love and appreciation for our families could be compared to our love and appreciation for breathing; it is part of who we are.

This book is a product of years of relationships with comrades in ministry. It begins with our mutual appreciation for the faculty and staff of Multnomah Biblical Seminary who model a love for God's Word and a love for the church.

For Tim, extra thanks go to

- Dr. Roger Trautmann for his passion for the work of ministry
- The Reverend Bob Chin for his zeal and love for the church

- Dr. Charley Bradshaw for coaching me in leadership principles
- Leaders and staff at Palm Springs Baptist Church from 1980–1990 for their loving hearts and lives of faith
- The staff members at the Luis Palau Association who have labored with me in various parts of the world to make Jesus Christ known over the past fifteen years

For Allen, extra thanks go to

- Dr. Tim Robnett, my coauthor and teacher
- Lynn Wiley, who holds me accountable
- Rick and Darcy Battershell, my partners in ministry and my exhorters
- Troy Anderson, my partner in ministry
- Lee Forstrom, my pastor who started me down the new adventure
- Dr. Donald Brake and Dr. Larry Ayers, who helped me open doors of ministry
- Dr. Ron Frost and Dr. Paul Metzger, who opened my eyes to God's great love
- Bill and Adele Larsen, the soft spot to land when we are hurting
- Dr. Richard Reeves, who helped me to discover God's vision for me
- Paul Rhoads, who moved me from head to heart
- Bob Barnes and Les Toews, my witnesses in my ownership transfer to God

We will never be able to say "Thank you!" enough to the forty editorial reviewers who critiqued our early drafts, and to David Sanford and the editorial team at Sanford Communications, Inc., who helped us revise and shape the final drafts.

INTRODUCTION

We thank God for Ray C. Stedman, Joe Aldrich, Luis Palau, and other wonderful Christian leaders and mentors who have demonstrated to us the truth of Jesus' words:

> You know that those who are regarded as rulers of the Gentiles lord it over them, and their high officials exercise authority over them. Not so with you. Instead, whoever wants to become great among you must be your servant, and whoever wants to be first must be slave of all. (Mark 10:42–44)

According to Jesus, Spirit-led believers and Christian leaders are first and foremost a "slave of all."

What does it mean to be Spirit-led? It is the opposite of doing things our own way. For instance, the Spirit of the Lord works in highly personal ways, but most of us want to use the latest methods. The Holy Spirit primarily focuses on transformation of the soul, but most of us seek the approval of others.

Through thirty years of vocational Christian ministry, I (Tim) hate to admit how much has been the work of my flesh, not the ministry of the Spirit of God.

Still, I stand amazed that God is doing a wonderful work in our world today! He is building his church. People are being reached with the gospel. Individuals, families, churches, cities, and nations are discovering in new ways the life of Jesus Christ through the ministry of the Holy Spirit of God.

Along with coauthor Allen Quist, I long for more of my every moment to be filled by the Spirit of Jesus Christ. I long for churches to be aware and empowered by the Lord of the church leading and freeing the church to enjoy his presence.

God has used Allen and me to serve the church through gifts of administration. It is our experience that those gifted in this way are often viewed as somehow void of the Spirit's working and power. It is as if the Holy Spirit empowers counselors with discernment, preachers with eloquence, evangelists with persuasion, but leaves other leaders to work in the flesh.

Our perspective is that the flesh (as described by the apostle Paul in the book of Galatians) potentially works through any Christian given to that power. Likewise, we believe the Spirit works in all believers.

It is our conviction that there is a tremendous need in the church today for those gifted in administration to be filled by the Spirit of Christ and to be allowed to serve the church with their giftedness so that, as Paul said to the churches of his day, the church may be orderly and productive (Titus 1:5; 1 Cor. 14:39–40).

After serving as a pastor for more than a decade, working in evangelism with the Luis Palau Association worldwide for more than sixteen years, and teaching at a biblical seminary for eight years, I have discovered what I believe the church needs to rediscover: A life lived without (apart from) the filling of the Holy Spirit is highly conflicted and unproductive for the kingdom of Jesus Christ.

Our desire, then, is to call the church back to exploring and obeying the voice of the Spirit of Jesus Christ in what we do and how we live and serve the church. Our prayer is that we may discover or rediscover the joy of the filling of the Spirit as a community of believers.

Many people have asked me (Allen) why I left banking, went to seminary, and dedicated so much of my time to ministry. Frankly, when I get tired, I sometimes ask myself the same question! Usually, though, I am having the time of my life.

One day, I was driving home from my day of work at the bank thinking about performance appraisals and wondering what it would look like if I received one from God. I decided that if I were God, I would fire me! I was busy doing stuff for God, but I was not in a hearing relationship with him. My thoughts were frequently about me doing well. I tried to be a spiritual hero in my story rather than a pawn in God's story. It was devastating—a time to do something drastic. My wife and I sold the stuff we did not need, including our house, and jumped in over our heads at seminary. We did not do it to get better at "doing stuff for God," but to let him teach us to live in him. That began our exciting adventure.

What is God doing now? Through attorney Troy Anderson, CPA Rick Battershell, and me, God launched a ministry to provide legal, tax, and management training for churches. God sends me church leaders who, like my wife and me, recognize that their individual lives, or the life of their church, are not working well and want help—usually through a leadership retreat. Jesus Christ varies my days with a peppering of opportunities, such as working with a church plant, as well as counseling, coaching, mentoring, and assisting new works for God. Now we believe God wants to use us to bring a message to the churches through this book.

As Tim and I got to know each other and started spending many hours together a few years ago, we discovered that we have a common burden for the church of America. We hurt with the 80 percent of churches that are in a condition of plateau or decline.[1] These churches either are not aware of their condition or they are aware and don't know the cause or the way out.

Is There Hope?

In the context of our ministries, we encounter many churches each year. Regardless of venue, we find a common struggle, a struggle that may be plaguing you or your church.

The chairman of an elder board, whom I'll call Thomas, told me (Allen), "We have a battle going on between a pastor and our elder board."

I asked him, "Are there any other conflicts among leadership?"

"Well, yes. It is far more complicated than first blush. There is a battle between a number of elders and deacons as well as the pastor."

By the time we finished drawing lines between the individuals in conflict, we could hardly see the diagram anymore. How could God heal that mess?

A pastor I'll call John commits adultery, spinning the congregation into turmoil. A number of the members go ballistic, wanting blood—some leave. Pastor John is devastated and desires restoration, but those who want blood want no part of restoration. What tension! How could God knock down that wall?

A recent seminary graduate I'll call Greg, and his wife, Florence, cry out to God all night. After only eighteen months, Greg had been let go by the board. Greg and Florence were sure that this little country church in a town of five thousand was the place God wanted them, even though they had been warned to be careful. The church has had eight pastors come and go in the last fourteen years. Some, like Greg, had been fired, and some had left in disgust. On top of everything, a number of members walked away, weakening the opportunity to change the leadership board causing the problems. How could God put new life and vision into this church?

Jerry, an associate pastor of a church with three hundred members (one that's not in decline, but not really going anywhere), addresses a congregational business meeting. "Christ is calling us to reach our community for him in a significant way," Jerry tells them. "We have maybe ten people give their life to Christ each year in this church. Eight to nine of those are children of our own families. We need to make some major changes in how we are doing church."

Carroll, a member, agrees with Jerry and says, "I think we are too inward-focused and need to make the changes to become a safer place for the unchurched to come."

The meeting chairman asks, "How many here feel this way?"

There is a small but committed number of people who feel strongly enough about this that they are willing to be part of it.

David, the senior pastor, stands up and says, "Look, this is just too big a change. We might lose some families if you few push it. So let's just table this and bring it up some other time."

There is an ugly battle, featuring words like backslider, rebellious to leadership, sinner, backstabber, troublemaker, head in the sand, ignorant, stupid, etc. It looks like it may be a split rather than a rebirth or a church plant. How could God get a hold on this church?

Amy is a single mom, struggling to make life work while living in the core area of a big city. She doesn't know God and knows it. Amy is having coffee with her friend Jenny, a believing single mom who is attending a big-city church near where they live.

Amy vents. "Look, Jenny, when I come to your church there are a lot of people but nothing is happening. There is nothing going on. You guys say you're there to help and serve but you don't do anything."

Jenny, wanting to offer something, responds. "Yes, I know it is difficult these days. I think that part of the problem is that the guys in charge haven't a clue what it is really like here."

"Why not? Can't they see?"

"I don't think that's the thing. I don't think they really want to see. None of them even live down here anymore."

Looking deep into Jenny's eyes, Amy digs. "There is a church just starting up down the street that cares. Except they're broke. They're trying to help, but they don't have any money and only a few folks."

"Yes, I've heard about them. I guess that's sort of how it goes. Those who have, won't. And those who can't, try."

God must look at this and shake his head. How could God kindle a fire for his passion to serve the inner city among the whole body of Christ?

What we have pictured is a description of much of the American church. Do you relate to any of these situations? Do any of these situations describe your life or the life of your church? Where is God in these situations?

WHY THIS BOOK?

There have been many books written on the subjects of Christian management and leadership. The material that has been written seems to be weighted toward issues of management and leadership based on the experience and knowledge of the authors. These books have presented many good ideas that are useful to readers in management and leadership—good ideas that can be applied to both Christian and non-Christian applications.

We believe that these books are still lacking. Whether intentional or unintentional, they do not leave readers with the impression of the need for faith and the leading of the Holy Spirit as a precursor to the type of humble, God-reliant leadership and management to which God has called his children. The Western world has a plethora of leadership principles, many of which are useful, and not necessarily biblical. Having the knowledge and skill to produce beautiful music does not necessarily mean that it will be produced for God's glory. It may be for man's glory.

The purpose of this work is to examine what Scripture says about leadership and management explicitly and implicitly. We intend to show how Scripture relates to "living by the Spirit," God's ownership, our role as servants and stewards, and God's children—all issues of faith. We want you to discover, as we have, that the control of the Spirit, our love relationship with God, and the life of faith are central to all aspects of management and leadership.

A number of specific Bible references are pivotal in this presentation. Paul made a point to the Romans that anything not done in faith is sin (Rom. 14:23). Paul exhorted the Galatians to live by the Spirit (Gal. 5:16). Paul directed the Colossians to do everything in the name of God and for God's glory, not for men (Col. 3:17–23).

Our Prayer

We have been praying that God would use this book in two ways. First, that he would use it as a wake-up call to the church that God is offering to individuals and congregations an abundant life of adventure, passion, and faith. Second, that he would teach us how infinite and enduring is his love for us. How strongly he wants us to crucify or abandon all that holds us so tightly to our safety and routine. How he is calling to us, "[insert your name or the name of your church], where are you?" This is the same call he made to Adam after Adam and Eve decided to try to make life work without God.

Our promise is to present our heart to you, the reader; to give to you hope that you and your congregation can have a life filled with adventure that requires a growing faith; and to show you and your congregation that God is not committed to your success or the success of your church, but to the success of his good news, and that he will use you in a greater way if you will let him.

We have provided discussion points at the end of the book to help you get into the material individually and as a leadership team.

May God bless and use this material
for his purposes and for his glory in your
life and the life of your congregation.

PART ONE

WHO IS LEADING THE CHURCH?

CHAPTER 1

FROM DEATH TO LIFE

Above all things keep in mind the Lord and handle everything in love.

—HEINRICH HAGELGANZ

It was a cold afternoon in north Portland, Oregon, compounding the sadness of a group gathered around the dying body of a friend. The word "friend" failed to capture their feelings, for this one was more than a friend, more than a neighbor, and in many ways more than family. This friend was the foundation of stability in their unsteady world, a source of strength when they grappled with forbidding helplessness, and an anchor in their times of storm.

As they all stood around their friend, all they could think was "why?" Why was this happening? How did the condition get this bad? How could they have missed the symptoms? Perhaps if they had paid more attention they could have done something. Was there anything they could still do to save their friend?

Try as they might, the group could not answer those questions about their friend, the Central Evangelical Church, and no one could deny the end was likely near.

I (Allen) was at that meeting with Central's leadership team when I asked, "When do you think you'll have to close your doors for good?"

"What do you mean close our doors?" someone responded.

"How many people do you need to keep doing ministry?"

"Wow, that's a tough question. I guess if we cut it back to the bare bones we would need at least thirty-five."

"What was your average attendance each of the past three years and this year?" I asked.

"It was seventy-nine, seventy-one, sixty-five, and fifty-six."

"Given that rate of decline, when do you think that you will reach thirty-five?"

"About three years—maybe less," was the reluctant response.

"Once you drop below thirty-five, what impact will that have?"

"I suppose it means then we will have to close our doors and pass this building and land on to some other church or nonprofit."

We paused as the leaders contemplated their situation. Then I asked, "How do you feel about that?"

One of the leaders, Willis Krieger, responded with anguish in his eyes, "This is the obvious conclusion, but it can't be possible. This is the only church I have ever known."

How It Began

In its infancy, the Portland church burst with adventure. It began on June 22, 1913, when a group of German immigrants, Georg Hohnstein, Conrad Wacker, Ludwig Deines, and Christian Baecker, founded the Second German Congregational Church with the help of fiery gospel preacher the Reverend Heinrich Hagelganz.

Not realizing the prophetic nature of his words, Hagelganz wrote in a church journal, "We advised the brothers, above all things, keep in mind the Lord and handle everything in love."

The Reverend Hagelganz agreed to be their "spiritual adviser" as long as he could continue to serve as pastor at his Beaverton congregation as well. He traveled to Portland every second Sunday.

"From all sides there was opposition to reckon with," Hagelganz wrote, "but none [of the organizers] reneged about continuing with the project. At all times, thanks to the strength of the brothers working together, the Lord soon allowed us his honor to celebrate the victory."

Believing that God would bless their efforts, later that summer the small group stepped out in faith to buy a lot on Northeast 8th Avenue and Skidmore Street, agreeing to spend four thousand dollars to build a new church. To highlight their faith they placed an inscription at the front of the sanctuary, words that spoke from their hearts: *We Preach Christ and Him Crucified.*

Hagelganz wrote, "For the collection to finance this building, the members supported the project very well and so the work of the Lord continued to be blessed. Since the number of members increased all the time, God's house quickly became too small."

In 1921, responding to the needs of a rapidly growing Sunday school, once again this young congregation ventured out. They added thirty more feet to the main sanctuary and built a basement under the entire building.

Like all fledgling churches, they faced many challenges, including the generational conflict between older German-speaking adults and the English-speaking younger generation, as well as a conflict between German and American cultures. However, fire for God fueled a growing church. By 1927, the next generation of leaders was not only serving Second German Congregational Church, but also ministering in other Portland churches. They were a forerunner to the church-plant and church-help movements of today.

Caution! Danger Ahead

As the once adventurous group adjusted to changing conditions both within and outside their congregation, seasons of growth mixed with seasons of decline. Through the years, the church gave birth to pastors, missionaries, and spiritual leaders in the community. They embraced the Christian Businessmen's Association, the start of the Portland area Youth for Christ, and more.

By January 1961, they found themselves pinned into a box. They needed a much larger church building because the location that had given them so many wonderful years now prevented them from expanding. Always willing to take risks for God, they ventured outward to northeast Portland and bought a two-acre piece of ground on which the men built the larger church, where they remain today, while changing their name to Evangelical Congregational Church.

The name changed but their mission for Jesus Christ did not. For years, the church poured itself into northeast Portland, continuing to touch families for our Lord. They were productive years, writes church historian Joanne Green Krieger. She calls them, "years of vital ministry."

As we look to the past, our hindsight is excellent. We wish we could go back and advise the leaders to beware! Prosperity opens the door for self-reliance, the risk of stepping out of a dependency on God. Our thoughts would echo the prophetic advice of Heinrich Hagelganz: "Above all things, keep in mind the Lord and handle everything in love."

Two large dangers loomed over them. First, the next generation of leaders was stepping into leadership, and second, the new community around them was rapidly growing, and the makeup of the population was changing. Church leaders needed to "keep in mind the Lord," staying sensitive to what God's Spirit was asking them to do to adapt to the changes in the community.

CONFLICTING AFFECTIONS

Sadly, as leadership transferred to the third generation, everything started downhill. The church lost touch with their neighbors and with what God wanted the church to do with his good news. While they did not mean to, sharing their faith dissolved into a good intent for someday soon. Too many other things got in the way—jobs, families, hobbies, cars. We have discovered that believers will pursue what or whom they have the greatest affection for. Sadly, affection for God often takes second place to affection for the things of this world.

Willis Krieger has his story of pain and disappointment, watching the slow death of the only church he had known. "In the early years," Krieger says, "we had revivals and growth. People were committing their lives to a lifetime walk with Jesus, which was obvious in their everyday lives. People worked and were successful because God made them successful. However, my generation just did not have the fervor. They did not have a commitment. They were into their own careers and houses and vacations."

Willis goes on. "I was part of a group of fifteen young families, and today my wife and I are the only ones left of that fifteen. Much of the decline was from people pursuing their careers and not knowing how to do that and still walk with Jesus. We were just sort of keeping on." For those families, affection for God became second place behind the affairs of life, despite the apostle Paul's warning, "No one serving as a soldier gets involved in civilian affairs—he wants to please his commanding officer" (2 Tim. 2:4).

Heading into the 1970s, as the new leadership assumed a greater influence, the church fell deeper into a "keeping on" lifestyle and "doing church" the same week after week. New people seldom visited; if they did visit, they did not return.

Please keep in mind that these are good people—they did not intentionally put the church into this decline. They unknowingly fell into the trap of not noticing what was happening around them, or if they did get a hint, it was not strong enough to make them do something about it.

You can imagine what it was like. Over the years, everything was the same, only getting smaller—smaller Christmas programs, fewer children, fewer adults, and almost no visitors. Potlucks and worship services all stayed the same. They put on the same bake sales selling the same stuff to the same people to raise money for the same missionaries.

People call it routine—and it is deadening. Habits and traditions take over, and people slide away from a sensitivity to the passion of our Lord. The unpredictable Spirit-led life filled with adventure for God gives way to the comfortable, and few think twice about it.

Sadly, no one questions whether all this "church stuff" is what God wants. No one compares what God has said to what the church is doing. How easy it is to turn extrabiblical tradition into something that people believe God would never change.

Through the eighties, during the years when John Schneider was pastor at the Evangelical Congregational Church, some young families came, at least enough to offset the loss of the elderly members. However, with the young people came tension between the two age groups. The younger members wanted to make changes in areas such as the music, outings, and neighborhood use of the building. The older members who held the purse strings liked it the way it was. The gulf within the church was beginning to look like the Grand Canyon. This condition could not continue, and it did not.

ANALYSIS TIME?

In 1994, the pastor left, followed shortly afterward by the exit of the young families, leaving the older generation to keep on "keeping on." If there was going to be an eye-opening experience for these good people, this would have to be it. However, it was not.

Because it was hard to find a pastor to lead them, for nearly two years they made do with interim pastors and pulpit supply. The church continued to get smaller—only now more rapidly than before. These older saints were feeling more and more desperate.

What could they do?

What they *did not* do was go to God, expecting that God might teach them about the cause of their problem. What they *did* do was look only at the two symptoms, the declining number of attendees and the empty pulpit, and make what many people would have thought was a reasonable decision.

Pastor Tom Lyman explains, "They reached out to the Central Free Methodist Church, an aging church like theirs only with a young pastor. They merged their two churches, accepting the Free Methodist pastor as the pastor of the new church, now called Central Evangelical Church. That way they could solve both problems at once. But still they did nothing differently in how they did church." In other words, they kept on "keeping on."

TIME TO STOP THE INSANITY

If "insanity" is doing nothing differently, but expecting change, then Central Evangelical Church must have been getting close to it. Rather than aligning their hearts with God's heart and allowing the Holy Spirit to lead them out of the decline, they allowed the downward slide to continue.

They were forgetting God's passion for lost people and for the growth of his followers, and unintentionally becoming an unattractive place for unbelievers to seek God. They were unattractive to those who wanted to be in an environment that encouraged a closer walk with God. When you are in a rut, it is hard to recognize what is happening.

Peter Drucker writes, "Nonprofits are prone to become inward-looking. People are so convinced that they are doing right, and are so committed to their cause, that they see the institution as an end in itself. But that's a bureaucracy. Soon people in the organization no longer ask, 'Does it serve God's mission for us?' They ask, 'Does it fit our rules?' And that not only inhibits performance, it destroys vision and dedication."[1] These words describe the condition of Central Evangelical.

However, Central Evangelical Church was not a typical body of aging members. They had a heritage of a God-loving, God-dependent people with a passion for God's passion. Unfortunately, Central Evangelical was merely living in the memory of their heritage.

This brings us back to the scene at the beginning of this chapter. As the leadership team stood around their dying friend, unable to figure out what had gone wrong, no one could deny the end was likely near.

GETTING RID OF THE SACRED COWS

After looking around the room, Willis added, "This is frightening."

"Willis, this is not an unusual story," I said. "Win Arn wrote that four of five [churches] are either plateaued or declining.[2] Your situation has become an epidemic in many American churches today."

Willis asked, "What could we do?"

"I don't know," I replied. "I suggest all of you ask God. Why not take your future to God, but with the clear understanding that everything—all that you have been clinging to in how you 'do church'—is on the altar for God to change."

George Barna wrote, "The successful churches we studied had no sacred cows."[3] Resolving to get rid of sacred cows was exactly what the leaders of this elderly church did. Pastor Tom Lyman met with the congregation immediately during the following Sunday service, presenting to them the prediction that they would likely have to close their doors within three years if they did not make some drastic changes.

THE TURNAROUND

The congregation committed a whole month to prayer. They held a monthlong prayer vigil combined with evening corporate prayer times. People prayed for God's mind and leading, and they prayed for a listening heart, willing to let go of whatever was holding back Central Evangelical. Of course, they realized it would not be easy. The decision to step out for God does not lower the temptation to be independent from God.

George Barna writes, "In most of the churches I've worked with or studied that have plateaued or are in decline, certain of the church's ministries are off-limits for review or discussion. Perhaps it is the quality of the pastor's preaching. Maybe it is the appearance of the buildings and grounds. Sometimes it is the nature of the worship service, or the productivity of the staff."[4]

It was a strong wake-up call!

To make no change meant the church would close its doors, and that was scary!

Yet to stop the death of their church meant a major change had to take place. They could no longer think that somehow, without doing anything differently, everything would get better. That was equally scary!

On June 6, 2002, immediately following Central Evangelical Church's month of prayer, Doug Frazier, the pastor of Northeast Community Church, abruptly startled Tom with a simple question during a lunchtime discussion: "What if our churches were to unite?" Northeast rented the church on Saturday nights, so it seemed like God had been pulling the two together. Could this be what God meant for them? Tom knew his congregation and how big an impact this would have. This was not like the merger they tried in 1996 that fell short of refocusing Central Evangelical. These were young people with young ideas and a young pastor fully backed by his young congregation.

There were so many decisions. How would God want each church to adjust for the two to come together? Both churches understood the struggle between walking in the Spirit and following the desires of the flesh; living God's way instead of "my way" (Gal. 5). Both churches had to come to grips that they might be forming a new body much different from what either church had been. Were they willing to accept that much change?

This was no small issue. It was the same issue that Joshua and God's people faced as God led them across the Jordan and to the walls of Jericho and on through the many battles they would have to fight. Would they believe God and let God lead the adventure, or would they try to keep control, staying self-dependent?

In the 1996 merger, Central Evangelical did not even consider giving up anything. The thought that God wanted them to rethink what they were doing did not occur to them. They must have known the church life was not well. They did not rethink it in 1996—could they do so now?

I am convinced the answer to that question would have been a big *no*—if God had not prepared all the parties to this decision.

VICTORY OR DEFEAT?

There were enormous issues looming over them. Both Northeast and Central Evangelical would have sacrifices to make. The first major issue both churches faced was that both were going to move from congregation-led churches to an elder-led church. This meant the control was moving from the people to the elders, and they would be relying on the elders to listen to and obey God. This seems simple enough, but it involves people giving up power and control, and few people are willing to do that—unless the Spirit takes over.

There were also sacrifices each would uniquely have to make.

NORTHEAST SACRIFICES	CENTRAL EVANGELICAL SACRIFICES
• Freedom to make changes quickly	• Safety of familiar faces
• Completely young leadership	• Control of music
• An older generation to care for	• Control of the kitchen
• Shared pulpit	• Loss of predictable routine
	• Quietness

The second major issue, more so for Central Evangelical, was dealing with the transitions. William Bridges writes, "There can be any number of changes, but unless there are transitions, nothing will be different when the dust clears.... Transition is different. The starting point for transition is not the outcome but the ending that you will have to make to leave the old situation behind."[5]

Consider the kitchen. How would we feel if, after living fifty years in a house, a friend moved in and suddenly shared our kitchen? We cannot find the saltshaker because someone put it in the wrong place. There is food we do not like in the cupboard. The ice cream is gone, and we are sure there was a little left the last time we had some. It seems trivial, but surrendering ownership to the church kitchen is a huge step.

Are we willing to do whatever God leads for the sake of the gospel at the level the apostle Paul writes about in his letter to the Corinthians?

> Though I am free and belong to no man, I make myself a slave to everyone, to win as many as possible. To the Jews I became like a Jew, to win the Jews. To those under the law I became like one under the law (though I myself am not under the law), so as to win those under the law. To those not having the law I became like one not having the law (though I am not free from God's law but am under Christ's law), so as to win those not having the law. To the weak I became weak, to win the weak. I have become all things to all men so that by all possible means I might save some. I do all this for the sake of the gospel, that I may share in its blessings. (1 Cor. 9:19–23)

A healthy church will abandon whatever Christ calls them to give up for the sake of the gospel.

Though seemingly rare, the leaders of Central Evangelical Church and of Northeast Community Church were willing to refocus their affections away from their own agendas, self-interests, comforts, and safety to the person of Jesus Christ. The congregations of both churches enthusiastically voted, "With God's help, Yes!" "Yes" on embracing a new work. "Yes" on letting the Spirit lead them into unknown territory. "Yes" on living their lives on fire for God instead of coasting in comfort.

When I first met the leadership team of Central Evangelical Church, discouragement, weariness, and defeat showed in every face. Since their bold decision to unite with Northeast Community Church, these same elderly leaders have a new look. There is life and excitement and anticipation for God's continuing work in their lives and their new church, Word of Life Community Church.

Look at what God has done. He has taken a group of young families with the determination and courage to start a new work and united them with a group of senior believers with the courage to restart a work for Jesus Christ. Which takes more courage? Which is the greater sacrifice? I do not know. I must admit, however, that when I stop and ponder the work that God has done in the hearts of the leaders and congregation of Central Evangelical, tears come to my eyes. These special saints have touched the heart of God.

"I think that it is amazing," Doug Frazier recalls. "Here is a group of older people that when I first met them I thought, 'This is going to be a difficult journey.' Yet in just a few months, they opened themselves up to new territory, and everything that once provided safety they tossed in the trash."

"The 'Self' had to step aside," says Willis Krieger. "I know for me and Adam [Bihn] that was not an easy decision because this church was the only church we ever knew. It was the Holy Spirit who worked in our hearts and the hearts of these people." Back came the words of the Reverend Hagelganz, "Keep in mind the Lord and handle everything in love."

Willis shared at one of our more recent meetings: "I have a new problem. Since we have been listening to God and pursuing his passions, we have been having more guests, and those guests have been staying. Now there are a whole lot of people I do not know yet. I guess that is a good problem."

WHERE IS THIS GOING?

When leaders and members of a church fall into routine and nonbiblical traditions, tall walls go up that limit the Holy Spirit, whom God never intended for us to limit. Our life in Christ (or as Paul puts it in Galatians 5—live by the Spirit) is dynamic and fluid, not locked into predictability or our control. Word of Life Community Church is now learning what it means to be walking in the Spirit.

The rest of this book is our attempt to focus the reader on the relationship of Christian leaders to the person of Jesus Christ, bringing attention to leadership and management implications. These implications center on a dependent love relationship with Jesus Christ and the return to his sovereignty in the real and practical areas of our lives and the life of the church.

CHAPTER 2

THE PULL OF CONFLICTING AFFECTIONS

E very Christian can identify with the tension Willis Krieger felt between letting God lead the church and trying to do the job on his own. This tension is between our affection for Christ—made clear by his Spirit leading and empowering us—and the insidious, deceptive affection for life in the flesh. Most of the time we are unaware of the struggle or its influence on our lives.

THE FLESH VERSUS THE SPIRIT

What is "the flesh"? Physically, it is just what it says, our flesh—our skin, muscles, organs, blood, and bones. Then there is the spiritual application. The flesh has been described as "[p]roneness to sin, the carnal nature, the seat of carnal appetites and desires, of sinful passions and affections whether physical or moral."[1]

The flesh surfaced back at the Genesis account of humanity's fall. The serpent said to Eve, "'You will not surely die.' ... For God knows that when you eat of it your eyes will be opened, and you will be like God, knowing good and evil" (Gen. 3:4–5). Adam and Eve believed the lie of the serpent, and they chose to try to be like God, to be autonomous, to make life work on their own without God.

Since the fall, humanity has continued to wish to be like God—self-existent and autonomous, trying to make life work without God. (Perhaps hell is God giving man what he wants, eternity without him.)

The Spirit, in contrast with the flesh, is the third person of the Godhead. The Spirit is the one Jesus promised to his disciples. He is the one who convicts us of sin and helps us live godly lives.

THE TENSION

What is the tension? In Paul's letter to the Galatians, the apostle tells us there is a war in our hearts between our affection for God's Spirit and our affection for the flesh:

> But I say, walk by the Spirit, and you will not carry out the desire of the flesh. For the flesh sets its desire against the Spirit, and the Spirit against the flesh; for these are in opposition to one another, so that you may not do the things that you please. (Gal. 5:16–17 NASB)

The Galatians were caught up with the law, and Paul attacked that entrapment. He questioned who was leading their lives and the life of the church—God or man in his flesh.

In today's world, our independent and self-dependent spirit destroys a Spirit-led life in the church. We respect skill over spiritual connectedness to God. We measure success based on the numbers of people or the amount of money coming into the church. We choose programs based on how well they worked in other churches rather than specifically setting aside our opinions, asking God, and listening. We have redefined members of our churches into a resource.

We forget that humans cannot do a work of God. Only God can do a work of God!

We believe God is calling churches back to his leadership, to the sovereignty of Christ, to the place where we quit relying on programs or asking God to bless *our* plans. God is calling us to the place where we are simply asking him what his plans are … and then listening to what *he* tells us to do.

Jesus said, "I am the vine; you are the branches. If a man remains in me and I in him, he will bear much fruit; apart from me you can do nothing" (John 15:5). We can do many activities that look good and even seem blessed by God, but they are not a work of God because God did not direct us to do them. We busy ourselves with ministry but not necessarily the ministry God wants to do through us. Doing church ministry work is not necessarily God's work. But we keep trying.

One day when I (Allen) was a boy on the farm, my father asked me to clean the corrals: a very smelly job, complete with lots of flies and other bugs—some that bite. It was awful!

On my way down to the barn, I noticed the gate into the machine shed was in bad repair. It was decision time. Should I clean the corrals or fix the gate? I convinced myself that the gate was urgent and had to be fixed; so I took on the task of fixing it, deceiving myself that my father would be pleased and proud of my commitment to the well-being of the farm. He and Mom would probably brag to the neighbors about how clever their son was.

I doubt that he ever talked to the neighbors about it, but I do know that he talked to me—lectured me may be more accurate. He had asked me to clean the corrals, something he wanted done. However, I hated cleaning corrals so I somehow blocked the nagging truth in my heart and did something that was more acceptable to me while rationalizing that this was somehow for him.

What I did with the gate is the flesh in action. According to Paul, we deal with it all our lives. Central Evangelical Church was dealing with it, especially after they decided to let Christ be sovereign in every area in their church, even how they "do church."

Has it been a walk in the park for them? No way.

Has it been out of the ordinary? Definitely!

What Willis, Adam, and the others in Central Evangelical Church did was to step out of safety and into the adventure of a

Spirit-led life. They committed to being living sacrifices, to walking in the Spirit. Essentially, they decided to refocus their affections back on Jesus Christ. They asked God what he wanted them to do, and they listened to hear what he told them. (We will address listening in a later chapter.)

Every day when they get up, every time they meet, in all of their decisions, the battle continues. Today, whom will they respond to? Whom will we respond to?

What is new about their struggles now is that they know what the battle is! It is a lot easier to fight a battle when we know who or what the enemy is.

Can you imagine being part of a church like that? While unusual, it is not unique. Henry Blackaby's book *What the Spirit Is Saying to the Churches* is the story of God's work in another congregation that abandoned itself to the leading of the Spirit.

The point is if our congregation is going nowhere, or worse yet, if it is going "somewhere" and that somewhere is the "wrong where," read on. God hasn't changed. God is still in the transforming business, working in the lives of individuals and congregations that are willing to walk by his Spirit and let the Spirit lead them where God wants them to go.

The story of Word of Life Community Church did not start with Tom Lyman and Doug Frazier's discussions of a rebirth. It began many years before, with the struggles of Central Evangelical Church.

What was getting in the way? Why did the people stop hearing God?

It reminds me of how we often are as Christians. God has a passion for lost people, but we busy ourselves doing all kinds of ministry—good ministry—that keeps us too busy to listen to God's heart. Central Evangelical Church did that for years. Remember the potlucks and bake sales? They can both be good, but if they are keeping us busy, too busy to listen to God, perhaps we need to shut down the ovens.

This is apparent not so much in what we are doing when we are "doing church." It relates more to what we are not doing. We are not going to God with a receptive, listening heart, asking him what we should be doing in the day-to-day practical aspects of ministry. Or if we do go to God, we often lug along our own agendas, wanting to hear from God so we can decide who has the better plan. We ask for his will, but in our heart of hearts, we reserve the right to make the final decision. We want to decide whether we will clean the corrals or fix the gate, even though we know he wants the corrals cleaned.

IDOLS AND STUMBLING BLOCKS

> Then some elders of Israel came to me and sat down before me. And the word of the LORD came to me, saying, "Son of man, these men have set up their idols in their hearts and have put right before their faces the stumbling block of their iniquity. Should I be consulted by them at all? Therefore speak to them and tell them, 'Thus says the LORD God, "Any man of the house of Israel who sets up his idols in his heart, puts right before his face the stumbling block of his iniquity, and then comes to the prophet, I the LORD will be brought to give him an answer in the matter in view of the multitude of his idols, in order to lay hold of the hearts of the house of Israel who are estranged from Me through all their idols."'"
> (Ezek. 14:1–5 NASB)

The leaders of Israel went to Ezekiel because they wanted to hear from God, just like we go to God to hear from him. But essentially God told them that their idols (their affections for power, influence, approval, or recognition) were in the way. They were not asking God for his guidance with the intention of doing whatever it was that God directed them to do.

It is still happening today. We go to God asking for his will, yet we have our own idols of power, respect, approval, recognition, and safety, so we quietly and subtly keep the right to make the final decision. Certain programs, people, or traditions can become idols. Or we put limits on the answer. Or we don't go to God at all. You may have heard the saying "If you don't think you will like the answer, don't ask the question." Often in our hearts we know the answer to what would please God, so we do not ask.

This was the case for many years at Central Evangelical. They were satisfied with "doing church" the way they always had and therefore did not feel the need to ask any questions. But remember what happened once they did ask—with a heart willing to do whatever God revealed to them. They moved into the adventure of a God-directed life, both individually and as a congregation. Knowing God's will has a lot to do with whether we are willing to let go of all our idols and actually believe that God has the answer.

Henry Blackaby says this thinking is not popular. "Often, when I talk to others about God being present and active and involved practically like this in our work, someone will tell me I sound like a 'mystic,' like someone who isn't practical."[2] Yet Blackaby goes on to point out that all through the Bible, God deals with his children in practical ways.

We have such a hard time staying dependent on God. We work hard developing skillful people in our churches, and then point with pride at the ministries and programs they maintain.

It is easy to imagine life in Central Evangelical over the years of the church's decline. It is a familiar story lived out in tens of thousands of churches. We get up Sunday morning and dress in something that fits the expectations of our church culture. We go to church and sit in the same area of the auditorium, and the service follows roughly the same format each week. We sing out of a hymnbook, or sing choruses, or both. Pastors aim messages at the hearts of 80 percent of the members with the purpose of stimulating them to do more in the service of God. A little less than 20 percent of the members bury themselves in "ministry" for God, feeling guilty because they are not spending the quiet, unhurried time with God they know that God desires. A few quiet saints do walk before God on a moment-by-moment basis. Before and after the service, people smile at each other, putting on their victorious faces even though they may feel discouraged.

People come, usually from other churches, and people leave—it's been a long time since a visitor decided for Jesus Christ and stayed around. Occasionally someone gives his or her life to Christ, but when the church starts encouraging him to change certain behaviors, he simply quits coming. People think, *It's just as well they leave because the church has a reputation to uphold. I mean, what would people think?* We have redefined "holiness" into an appearance-and-behavior issue, minimizing the heart.

Does any of this seem familiar?

The average church could engrave volumes of tablets based on all the unwritten rules and expectations we impose on one another. In reality, no one ever identifies the rules and expectations, let alone places them against the measuring stick of God's Word.

There is never a time when we are not caught in the tension between the Spirit and the flesh for our affections, and therefore there is never a time when believers do not need to identify and crucify our idols and stumbling blocks. Yet there is little awareness of the struggle. Churches seldom do a spiritual triage. Central Evangelical didn't for years, not until the death of the church became imminent.

Seldom does the church address the real problem—the flesh. We focus on the symptoms and problems that are revealed (and they should be dealt with). This is like taking the temperature of a sick child, finding a fever, and solving the problem by putting the child in a bathtub of cold water. Yes, it is important to control the fever, but we also need to address the cause of the fever.

WHO IS IN CHARGE?

Paul gives us a gauge for measuring who or what is in charge, the flesh or the Spirit. He identifies specific symptoms of the flesh.

> When you follow the desires of your sinful nature, your lives
> will produce these evil results: sexual immorality, impure

> thoughts, eagerness for lustful pleasure, idolatry, participa-
> tion in demonic activities, hostility, quarreling, jealousy,
> outbursts of anger, selfish ambition, divisions, the feeling
> that everyone is wrong except those in your own little group
> ["factions," NIV], envy, drunkenness, wild parties, and other
> kinds of sin. (Gal. 5:19–21 NLT)

Most of us would like to believe that Galatians 5 only describes evil people. But Paul wrote this letter to Christians! Further, he wrote this letter to churches (or assemblies). While we are not suggesting that we should not interpret the Scripture individually, we are suggesting that we must also look at this corporately. Here is what we mean:

First, a church is made up of individuals and will therefore have a spiritual consensus or personality. We are all individuals, yet we are part of a greater body. When parts of our body are dealing with sin, the whole body is dealing with it. In a culture that prizes independence, this is hard to internalize and live out day to day.

Second, Paul wrote this letter to a group of churches (assemblies), and he meant it to be read to the congregations like a sermon. He can be speaking to both individuals and the church as a whole. Examples are the "one another" verses in chapter 5:

> For the whole Law is fulfilled in one word, in the statement,
> "You shall love your neighbor as yourself." But if you bite
> and devour one another, take care that you are not consumed
> by one another. (Gal. 5:14–15 NASB)

In this passage, Paul is addressing Christians as a group. It's the voice of a parent saying to his or her children, "Watch out or you're going to hurt each other."

Later, Paul uses the group pronouns "we" and "us" to address the assembly as a whole.

> If we live by the Spirit, let us also walk by the Spirit. Let us
> not become boastful, challenging one another, envying one
> another. (Gal. 5:25–26 NASB)

So clearly it's appropriate to interpret Galatians as a message to a church body rather than only to individuals. This has critical implications.

Church leaders should not ignore the tension between the Spirit and the flesh that Paul is addressing! While leaders are examining their individual lives, they also need to look at the congregation and ask, "Are we as a body of individuals truly seeking to walk in the Spirit with all the inherent risks of change that God may direct, or are we allowing affection for things of the flesh to influence some of our members to set the tone for the body?" Paul warns about that, too.

> You were running a good race. Who cut in on you and kept you from obeying the truth? That kind of persuasion does not come from the one who calls you. "A little yeast works through the whole batch of dough." (Gal. 5:7–9)

It is critical that church leadership remain *intentionally* on guard, seeking God's transforming Spirit in the life of the church to prevent the flesh from controlling it. In Galatians, Paul says to be protected against the flesh, we must be led by God through his Spirit. And Paul immediately gives a gauge to us as individuals and as an assembly to evaluate this Spirit-flesh tension.

> So I advise you to live according to your new life in the Holy Spirit. Then you won't be doing what your sinful nature craves. (Gal. 5:16 NLT)

The New American Standard Bible uses the words "walk by the Spirit." However we word it, if we walk (or live) in the transforming power of the Spirit of God, the power of the flesh will dwindle.

When there is immorality, bickering, gossip, or any number of other problems, we preach against them—as we should. Nevertheless, we often fail to address the cause of those issues: Our affection for ourselves (the flesh) usurps our affection for God.

As we see these symptoms of the flesh, we can sense who or what is in control of us either as individuals or corporately—the Spirit or the flesh. Although we do need to address the symptoms, we also need to look at the underlying cause of those symptoms. Paul is saying that when we follow the desires (affections) of our sinful nature, there will be obvious results.

"Sexual immorality," an endemic within the church, is ignoring the Spirit and trying to fill desires in ways not intended by God. God has called us to delight in him—to focus our affections on him. God loves us with his infinite and indescribable love, and he gives us the opportunity to receive that love and calls us to love him in return.

"Impure thoughts" are thoughts that are "alloyed," thoughts of a double mind—not the mind of a living sacrifice. "Eagerness for lustful pleasure" could be thought of as lustfulness. Even churches can corporately lust after stuff, such as edifices that are a testimony to man's glory and wealth.

"Consumerism" is the term that best describes our impatient society that is up to its neck in debt. Unfortunately, this term also applies to churches that must have all the latest things—a coffee shop in the foyer, plush chairs in the auditorium, a high-tech sound system—it can be anything that takes precedence over God's ministries.

Most Christians would like to limit "idolatry" to something like worshipping a statue or idol—something on the surface that is easy to avoid. But Paul helps us understand this word in Colossians 3:5 when he associates covetousness with idolatry. That sounds like materialism, doesn't it? Some churches have made their church buildings an idol.

The rest of the list—hostility, quarreling, jealousy, outbursts of anger, factions, envy, selfish ambition, and divisions describe many churches. The problems have become so prevalent that many organizations have started ministries to deal with individual and group conflict within churches. In fact, it was a division that triggered our first contact with Central Evangelical Church.

There is another side to the conflict: walking in the Spirit. This is a life with our affections focused on Jesus Christ, not just the ministry of Jesus Christ. The Spirit-led life is a life of dependency on God, a life of growing love for him and increasing obedience to him, flowing out of our love relationship with him.

Just as there is evidence of the flesh, there is evidence of the life of the Spirit (the fruit of the Spirit). The evidence is obvious in both individuals and churches.

In a Spirit-led church, we find contagious love—a love for God that results in a love for people. In a Spirit-led church, we will still find problems, suffering, losses, and frustration. But in those difficult times, we will find a peace and gentleness in the congregation that creates a strong sense of safety for visitors and new believers to be comfortable growing in Christ.

In Galatians, Paul describes the fruit of the Spirit: "love, joy, peace, patience, kindness, goodness, faithfulness, gentleness, and self-control" (5:22–23). When a church truly seeks to live out these attributes, it is a Spirit-filled church. Our desire is for this to be true of our churches!

CHAPTER 3

DISCOVERING A LOVING AND TRANSFORMING GOD

In the last chapter, we ended by describing what we hope your church is—a church that, even during problems, remains led by God through his Spirit. Those churches come in all sizes: large, small, and in between. We can find them in big, small, and medium-sized communities. The leaders of those churches have a grade-school, high-school, trade-school, college, or graduate-school education. They all love God, and it shows.

Unfortunately, only a minority of churches are fully Spirit driven. The remaining majority of churches are in plateau or decline. These churches vary in size, location, and pastoral education just like the Spirit-led churches. Some of them even have a great love for God. Others want their love for God to be their controlling passion, but unfortunately, are putting their affections on their houses, cars, hobbies, Internet, or televisions. And some leaders of struggling churches have not yet even recognized there is a problem.

Most leaders know that God wants to do a work in their hearts and the heart of their churches. And they know that someday they need to get more serious about it. However, Paul says that God wants leaders to get serious about letting him do his transforming work NOW. Paul says that God is serious about doing a major surgery on our minds.

> Therefore, I urge you, brothers, in view of God's mercy, to
> offer your bodies as living sacrifices, holy and pleasing to
> God—this is your spiritual act of worship. Do not conform
> any longer to the pattern of this world, but be transformed
> by the renewing of your mind. Then you will be able to test
> and approve what God's will is—his good, pleasing and per-
> fect will. (Rom. 12:1–2)

Society, including much of the contemporary church society, dilutes the scope and depth to which Paul calls Christ's followers. Many Christians, including leaders, relegate "living sacrifice" to a *segment* of their life, not all of it. Harry Blamires, in his book *The Christian Mind*, addresses this tendency to segment our lives. We can receive a truth from God and somehow are able to put that truth into our spiritual segment and not necessarily apply it to every part of who we are.

In the above Scripture, Paul not only addresses God's call for us to be "living sacrifices" and to be sacrifices that are holy (set aside for God) and pleasing to God, he also provides an understanding of how God makes that happen. Paul teaches that first the Christian must come to understand what "the pattern of this world" is and what God's pattern is. Then Paul explains that the process God uses is transformation of our minds. God is in the transforming business and he does it throughout the entire journey of our lives.

To begin this journey of transformation, we must begin taking some steps. And probably the most difficult part of any journey is the first steps. In fact, the first steps in this discovery time are not really steps at all. They are more like stops than steps. They mean getting off the carousel of life and just stopping. They mean gathering the leadership of your church and spending two or three months or more in regular prayer and study—study of God's love letter and manual for living, the Bible. These should be focused prayer and study times of rediscovering intimacy with Jesus Christ.

A NOTE TO LEADERS AND PASTORS: Please do *not* shortcut this process of "stops" by just teaching or preaching a study. *All* the leaders need to go through hours of study and prayer time together. As we study Scripture together, discussing what it is saying to us, we will want to pour out our hearts to God in praise, confession, commitment, and love. And we will want to do that many times. We will want to ask God to make us receptive to what he has to reveal to us.

The church needs to open itself up to God's leading, with an ear ready to listen and a heart freed from the influence of personal agendas. We may discover the leadership of our church chooses to make this a permanent part of their lives together.

First Stop—God's Passions

In this first "stop" toward transformation, we may focus on discovering or rediscovering what God's passions are. What is God's highest and second-highest concern or command? Or we may examine God's criticism of Israel and Judah that drove him to send his people into captivity. We might study Jesus' criticism of the Pharisees. What can we infer he wants from the church and us?

We may evaluate God's call of his children to a life given over to him—one that will include risk. We may find ourselves asking some questions. Are the persecuted churches and Christians just victims, or is persecution part of God's love plan? What does God want done with his good news? What is biblical worship?

We will come up with many more questions that we will want to find answers to through our study, discussion, and prayer. One section of Scripture will lead to another and another. Our discussions will lead to still more places in Scripture we will rediscover. During prayer, the Holy Spirit will lead us to verses we had not considered.

In this process, what we are doing is stopping long enough to take a new, fresh, and deep look at who God is and what pleases him. And we are doing it as a body of church leaders. It is amazing how little church leadership examines Scripture and their own hearts together. The hardest part of this first stop is to approach the process without our personal fears, agendas, or extrabiblical church traditions influencing the outcome. (We will be examining church traditions in a later chapter.)

Because fear, personal agendas, and extrabiblical traditions are so deeply entrenched in our lives and church cultures, it is difficult to recognize their influence. For churches, this tendency has caused many of the problems they are facing. God has called us to a life given over to him and he is *serious* about it. It is a life-and-death war with long-term implications. We need to take a serious look at who God is and what he wants from his children and his churches.

When our study is well underway, we will discover at a much deeper and more inclusive level that God is sovereign, that he loves us, and that he is committed to his good news. *His number one concern or command is that we love him* and that our lives show it. We are to teach the importance of this love of God to those we have influence over. We do this by the way we act, talk, and live out the Christian life. God is concerned about our affections. And he wants to be the focus of our affections.

His second concern or command is that we allow his love to flow through us to those around us, including our enemies and other difficult people. God is a pursuing lover, whose heart's desire is that we love him in return. Thus, our love for him expresses itself in our service, flowing from a heart of love rather than from duty or guilt.

We will probably discover the number one work he wants from us is to believe in him (that is to commit our lives and possibly deaths to him) and to be in such a deep, loving, committed, and dependent relationship with him that any suffering we meet will seem a joy to us because it is for him.

This is not a game or a merry-go-round ride. As we stop to consider God's character and pursue his passion, along with our church we will fall deeper and deeper in love with our sovereign Christ. We may find ourselves increasingly weeping when we are praying and increasingly aware of how little we know him, yet want more and more to know him deeper.

SECOND STOP—EXAMINATION

The second stop is also a discovery process. In this stop, we will be examining ourselves as individual leaders, our staff as a body of leaders, and the church as a whole. Again, the most difficult part of this stop is to be as open to God as we can. We will ask God to show us where we are consistent or inconsistent with what we discovered from our time of prayer and study with Christ.

It is so easy to fool ourselves here. We throw out clichés and phrases that we have learned in order to look and sound good. Even in our corporate church structure, we have bylaws and brochures that say what our bylaws and brochures are supposed to say. Christians, including church leaders, are good at putting on masks or being imposters in front of others—and maybe even themselves. We may already be aware of that in our own lives and the lives of other leaders. In our hearts, we may be struggling with this tension. If we are not already struggling with the tension, we may begin to struggle after God reveals a pride issue to us.

In this second stop, we will be letting the Holy Spirit examine us as leaders based on the reality of what is happening in our lives and in the church, not just what we say. We will be using the works of our lives and the life of our congregations to reveal our faith and affections.

In many churches, the primary concern leaders have with new Christians (and for that matter their own people) is that they look, talk, and behave in a predetermined way. That is not, however, the way God intends for his church to be.

Throughout the world, wonderful followers of Christ dress differently, behave differently, sing different music to different types of instruments, and worship differently. However, there is one characteristic common to all who have given themselves to God: the fruit of the Spirit—love, joy, peace, patience, kindness, goodness, faithfulness, gentleness, and self-control.

There seems to be a culture, perhaps we could call it a "kingdom of God culture," for those who love God with all their heart and all their soul and all their strength. This means that their affection for God is the driving affection for their life. To them, this kingdom culture is bigger than world cultures, bigger than Western rationalism, bigger than Eastern mysticism, bigger than modernism or postmodernism, and bigger than any church-ism that exists anywhere in the world.

THE MAIN THING

In Matthew 22:36–40, Jesus said that loving God is his primary concern for us. He wants his children to love him. We cannot command people to love God. We cannot teach them to love God with just words. People catch love for God from God through exposure to someone who loves God, someone whose love for him is obvious both verbally and nonverbally.

As leaders of our families and churches, we rely heavily on words. But words are the least effective communication tool when face-to-face with somebody—especially someone close to you.

Picture a young couple that has just gotten married and is at the beach on their honeymoon. They are so much in love. They have eyes only for each other. They are running around the shallow surf with their pant legs rolled up, laughing and giggling together. The groom reaches down and teasingly splashes water on his bride. Giggling back at him, she says, "Oh, I hate you. Take that," as she splashes water back on him.

What did she say? Her words were "I hate you." Given the facts, no one would conclude her real message was "I hate you." It was "I love you." She loved him and was simply enjoying a playful moment with her husband. Our nonverbal communication can sometimes say exactly the opposite of the words coming out of our mouths.

When Jesus said God's first commandment is that his children love him, Jesus was drawing from the Old Testament, specifically Deuteronomy 6:5–9. In that passage, God directs his children to pass on the love for God to others.

> Love the LORD your God with all your heart and with all your soul and with all your strength. These commandments that I give you today are to be upon your hearts. Impress them on your children. Talk about them when you sit at home and when you walk along the road, when you lie down and when you get up. Tie them as symbols on your hands and bind them on your foreheads. Write them on the doorframes of your houses and on your gates.

The word "children" in the passage can be a broad word covering just about anybody.

"Impress" comes from a word that means *whet* or *sharpen*. A synonym for "whet" could be "arouse or kindle." Both sharpening and whetting involve a great deal more than the use of just words. It involves all of who we are, including our values and affections. Here lies much of the problem.

The problem is that many church leaders, like other people, are caught up in houses, cars, jobs, looking good, being respected or liked, or being in control. Much of the time, we would have to infer that what they value most is not God.

Love takes time. Love takes communication, communication takes involvement, and involvement takes a lot of time. We praise God for the leaders who do take the time to love God and to display that love in their lives.

Most effort in churches is spent keeping programs going, yet God's heart is for a love relationship. This is a great discussion point and point of prayer, is it not? How do we as leaders keep "the main thing the main thing"? Of course, the first thing is that we, as a leader or body of leaders, personally make God the most important thing in our lives.

THE TENSION

Once we have a clearer picture of our loving God, what pleases him (what he wants from you), and how he is leading us to approach life and ministry differently, we will find increasing tension. That tension is between what we are learning that God wants from us and our strong habits or addictions to make life work on our own—managing the church but in our strength and our wisdom.

In the previous chapter, we already read about the flesh and its hold on us. And earlier in this chapter, we read about the fruit of the Spirit. In Galatians 5, Paul draws a picture of the flesh and the Spirit in conflict—a conflict that does not resolve during this lifetime. This is a real tension. This is not just theology. It is a real, practical problem, yet many leaders today miss the point of the problem.

The flesh is real and crippling, destroying churches and the lives of Christians. We are seeing it in church battles, church splits, leadership and congregational anger, conflict, and long-term hatred between congregational members. We see the flesh in the growing number of leaders and members of congregations falling into sexual affairs, sexual addiction, pornography, and divorce. We see the flesh in addiction to possessions, the idolatry of materialism, and selfish ambition. Sometimes church leadership even applauds our addiction to success when we perform well in ministry. We see the flesh in the rage that occurs at times in meetings or between people in conflict. We see the flesh in the various groups that fight with one another. We see the flesh in the homes of Christians as they invite strangers into their homes to do immoral acts in front of their family (also known as today's average television program).

We are beginning to see some churches attacking these issues. They are taking up support groups for the abused and the abusers. There is help for those suffering from addiction. Organizations like Crown Ministries are attacking materialism by helping people understand God's ownership. The organization Peacemakers is helping churches to learn how to mediate conflict. All of these battles against the symptoms of the flesh are good and need to happen. However, it is still missing the point. Dealing with the symptoms without dealing with the cause will simply result in the flesh sprouting up again in the same area or in some new area. Church leaders must deal with the root cause—the flesh itself. The flesh is that part of us that tries to make life work for us, to be autonomous or independent of God in the practical segments of our lives.

Leaders, how do we fight against the flesh? Paul says it is by walking or living by the Spirit. So again, we are back to God's main concern—that we love him with all our heart and all our soul and all our strength. His concern is that we are in a deep, dependent, obedient love relationship with our Lord. His concern is that we have him as our primary affection—that he is the center of and sovereign over our lives, not us. We need to let God lead the church and the members of the congregation that make up that church.

The flesh is an enemy of Christians and the church. To fight against that enemy we need our relationship with Christ to encompass all areas of our lives, our church leaders' lives, the congregation members' lives, and the corporate life of the church. It is walking and living in the Spirit.

THE THERMOMETER OF THE FLESH

The symptoms of the flesh that Paul outlines in his letter to the Galatians are like a thermometer. A thermometer tells us information about a current condition and may reveal the need to look for a deeper problem.

We notice that our child has a fever. Using a thermometer, we discover that his or her temperature is 105 degrees. We now know several facts. We know our child has an excessively high fever. We know from experience that we need to get the fever down to prevent bigger problems. We also know there is something causing our child to have the fever. And so we know that we must find out what it is that is causing the fever.

What do we do? We get the fever down using medication and cold water. Of course, we would never consider just stopping there. We would take further steps to find the cause of the fever by getting help from someone trained in medicine. We would deal with both the symptom and the cause of the fever.

The same principle applies to church leadership. We examine our own lives and the life of our congregation to find symptoms of the flesh, as discussed above. As we discover a symptom or symptoms (and we will, many times—they will be right in our faces), we know two facts. First, we know we have a symptom of the flesh that we must deal with. Second, we know there is an underlying cause—the flesh.

Of course, we must deal with the symptoms of the flesh—and do it God's way. Dealing with symptoms of the flesh is an enormously complex and sensitive process, one in which we need great care, prayer, and preparation. This cannot be overstated. Confronting issues of immorality, anger, discord, gossip, addictions, factions, rage, and the other symptoms of the flesh is risky. It carries the potential for great damage, pain, broken hearts, defeated lives, lawsuits, etc.

Even better than dealing with the symptoms of the flesh, don't we wish that we could stop the symptoms before they appeared? What if there was an immunization shot for the flesh? According to Paul, there is. His solution to the flesh is walking and living in a Spirit-directed, deeply dependent love relationship with our sovereign God. Therefore, the primary focus of all that happens in the church should be to point people in that direction—to bring the focus on Christ.

Would it not be best for church leadership to make the depth of their love for God the priority? In terms of the overall health of the congregation, is there anything more important than leadership itself building and preserving that Spirit-directed relationship with God and then passing that on to the congregation? Jesus says that this is God's priority. Shouldn't leadership have the same priority as God? It must begin with us as leaders.

We have been in many churches, and yet we can count on one hand the number of leadership groups (boards, etc.) that actively and practically make the growth and maintenance of their love relation-ship with God their priority. It is tragic. They must either assume that there is no battle and Paul is mistaken, or they must believe that they are so deeply mature in Christ that they are above risk. It sounds a lot like pride, doesn't it? Maybe this is the real reason that so many churches are in decline. Maybe church leadership is spending too much time wrestling with what *they* think is urgent, instead of what God calls the number one priority.

Be careful here. Our priority is falling deeper and deeper in love with God—for God himself. Our priority is not a deeper relationship with God for what we get out of it.

In the devotional *My Utmost for His Highest*, Oswald Chambers summarizes this priority in the devotion for March 12:

> Our motive for surrender should not be for any personal gain at all. We have become so self-centered that we go to God only for something from him, and not for God himself. It is like saying, "No, Lord, I don't want you; I want myself. But I do want You to clean me and fill me with Your Holy Spirit. I want to be on display in Your showcase so I can say, 'This is what God has done for me.'" Gaining heaven, being delivered from sin, and being made useful to God are things that should never even be a consideration in real surrender. Genuine total surrender is a personal sovereign preference for Jesus Christ himself.[1]

CHAPTER 4

SPIRITUAL LEADERSHIP

It was a shock! Nothing said in a year of monthly meetings prepared us for what we heard at a pastors' meeting in San Bernardino, California, in 1984. I (Tim) had been meeting with several pastors of the same denomination at a Bob's Big Boy for breakfast, to seek fellowship and just talk.

A few minutes into our monthly meeting, the announcement came. It must have been my ears playing tricks on me, but I think one of my fellow pastors blurted out, "I can't take it anymore. I resigned on Sunday and am looking for a new vocation." In all that time he had not said one word about his problems—not one single word. We had no clue he was under such pressure.

Not one word. Zip. No hint that he was suffering deeply from depression and a sense of worthlessness. Nothing—then suddenly, he gives up.

Church leaders, as all people, face dysfunctions inside and outside the church. Often we are perceived as people exempt from the pain and struggles of life. With a need to "be leaders," we hide behind the shield of pride and fear to keep the ugly realities of broken relationships, unmet goals, dry seasons in our walk with God, or melancholy days from overwhelming us.

The reality of effective leadership is this: Within the church, we need to be more honest about what can truly set the leader and the congregation free to let God's grace fill their souls and relationships. Leaders face a daily challenge to live in the power of the Holy Spirit.

In the last chapter, we spoke of the flesh affecting the church. For this force to have its insidious way within the church, we must assume that first it is an issue for leaders, and not just laypersons. "Every organization is a direct reflection of the leadership it has been given, for good or bad." Bobb Biehl shared this with me (Tim) more than twenty years ago, and his leadership maxim has highlighted the experience of my own journey. I have seen it play out in the lives of friends, students, and mentors, revealing the conflict of flesh and Spirit as common to all.

However, there is hope when we turn to the grace of God to unravel our litany of emotions, unanswered questions, and broken relationships. This grace will heal our souls as we journey toward God's plan for church leaders: transformational leadership. We will find that when leaders are filled by the Spirit of Christ, God brings healing and health through them to the church. When the leaders cultivate an environment of grace, then freedom comes into the relationships within the church and with everyone who is exposed to the church. An organic process spawns healthy relationships and a dynamic connection between God and his people. For some, the word *contagious* has summarized the energy of this process. Leaders filled by the Spirit of Christ provide transformational leadership for the church.

A Culture of Grace

Ray Stedman brought a culture of grace and forgiveness to thousands who enjoyed his relaxed leadership style during the tumultuous days of the 1960s and 1970s in Palo Alto, California. The Jesus Movement was just starting when a number of "their types" first walked through the doors of Peninsula Bible Church. Upper-middle-class folks turned their heads at these uniquely dressed, long-haired, free-spirited souls.

What would the church do? How would the church respond to this new breed? With warmth and affirmation, Ray welcomed and encouraged them to become part of the body of Christ in that place. A refreshing spirit swept away many of the doubts and fears of those church members with questions. Peninsula Bible Church became a haven and harvest field for the younger generation who were seeking God. Spiritual leadership brought integrity and love to those on both sides of a changing culture.

With a few powerful words, the apostle Paul emphasizes the utter necessity for the Spirit of Christ to empower personal relationships. "Do not get drunk on wine.... Instead be filled with the Spirit.... Submit to one another out of reverence for Christ" (Eph. 5:18, 21). Without this journey of submission to the leadership of God, we become destructive healers in a broken and fragmented world. This is not an option for leaders within the body of Christ. What empowers our thoughts, emotions, and volitions crafts the reality of relationships within the family and the church. Thank the good Lord that our relationship with him is not merely a matter of cognitive input or determination to "live for God." Rather it is a life characterized by his pursuing grace.

Spiritual leadership begins with those leaders who will recognize their utter dependence upon God. As they are learning what it means to "be filled with the Spirit" (Eph. 5:18), spiritual leaders must face the brokenness that comes by living in reliance upon their own human efforts apart from the empowerment of the Holy Spirit. These leaders find new joy in knowing the forgiveness of God and are quick to extend that forgiveness and grace to others.

Our egos and self-interest have gotten in the way of God's leadership on many occasions. This is particularly true in our roles as leaders. Many times we have failed to rely on the Holy Spirit and have become anxious, defensive, angry, and boastful. However, Holy Spirit–inspired leadership focuses on the healing and strengthening of others. It does not draw attention to itself or protect itself; rather, it seeks to serve and empower others.

A Distorted View of Leadership

I (Tim) remember the numerous times that I attended the carnival section of the Kern County fair in Bakersfield, California. One of my favorite attractions was the walkway of mirrors. This was a simple portable trailer with a number of mirrors crafted to distort one's appearance. One mirror showed me fat, another showed me tall, some mirrors gave me a big head and a small body. I did not understand the technology, but the effect was humorous.

Often what some call biblical leadership appears rather distorted, which is not humorous. These distortions come to us from various sources. Some are a product of popular culture. Others come from traditions in the church. Biblical leaders are a rare breed. Their leadership desires are challenged by the many views of what constitutes a spiritual leader.

In America, a business environment dominates us. Free enterprise and capitalism rank with baseball, apple pie, and the American flag as core values. As such, we often cannot distinguish between entrepreneurial-style leadership and biblical leaders. Donald Trump, on his TV show, *The Apprentice,* articulates the business model of leadership. There are educational models of leadership that emphasize process and collaboration. There are nonprofit models that seek to discover and resolve the social ills of society. However, we believe that these leadership models often fall short of the biblical norm.

What Is Biblical Leadership?

Jesus used two small, yet powerful, words in correcting the disciples' view of leadership. He uttered the phrase "not so" (Matt. 20:26). The disciples longed to be famous and powerful. The mother of James and John sought to position her sons in places of power (Matt. 20:20). She asked Jesus to have her sons sit on each side of him in his coming kingdom. Jesus said that was not his decision (Matt. 20:21–23). His emphasis was on his teaching to her and the disciples. It established a definition of leadership in his kingdom that was far different from how the world viewed leadership.

Jesus announced two startling dimensions within his kingdom. He began by first emphasizing that the "first will be last" (Matt. 19:30). He noted that, rather than seeking top positions, true biblical leaders ask, "How can we empower others?" *Empower* refers to the transformation that occurs when one integrates biblical truth into the normal patterns of life.

Second, Jesus emphasized that serving is what makes a leader great (Matt. 20:26, 28). The leaders in his kingdom will be servants of all. Rather than using a sword to symbolize leadership, Jesus chose a water basin and towel. With these tools, he washed the disciples' feet (John 13:1–7). This is a very different and seemingly unrealistic type of leadership in comparison with what we experience in the world today. These dynamic principles demand our constant attention. Many of us are not reflecting on or teaching these principles for the first time, but for the hundredth time. Yet, Jesus' kingdom is built on such truths and we need to recommit ourselves to his way.

WHERE ARE THE LEADERS?

The story of the early church indicates that leaders become evident to those they lead. Biblical leaders clearly demonstrate godly character. Biblical leaders have a reputation. Their lives demonstrate a transformation of heart. Christ's disciples were leaders who encountered the resurrected Jesus Christ. That encounter radically transformed their lives—and not just as a course in character development or leadership skills. Their priorities were radically adjusted and completely rearranged.

When ethnic discrimination expressed itself in the early church, the apostles asked those feeling the crisis to choose men "full of the Spirit and wisdom" (Acts 6:3) to help find resolution. The church was able to discern and select such men. They chose godly men who handled the situation with grace and wisdom and allowed the church to continue to grow and impact their world with the good news of Jesus Christ. This problem-solving ability didn't come from strong individuals doing their own thing. It was based on the work of the Holy Spirit through men yielding to his leadership.

Where are these leaders today? We wish we could say they are our pastors and the other leaders in our churches, but this is not always the case. Are we truly being led by his Spirit? The carnal mind can invade and control any Christian leader. We need to examine ourselves regularly and ask ourselves: What are we modeling and teaching? What do our corporate structures look like? How are our policies and procedures reflecting his way? What outcomes are we really concerned about?

Paul instructs his protégé Timothy, a young pastor, to be selective when asking others to serve with him in leading the church. Timothy, as we discern from the Scriptures, may have tended to be overwhelmed at times. He could have chosen anyone who was willing and available to provide leadership for the church. Yet Paul insisted that those who would provide leadership for the church must be godly, mature men, devoted to the task at hand.

A leadership criterion has been clearly articulated for the church in the Word of God (1 Tim. 3:1–13; Titus 1:5–9; Eph. 5:8—6:9). This criterion requires that the church take seriously the plan of God for leading his church. God views his church as a bride and uses terms of familial definition to focus our attention on the importance of relationships over tasks in leading the church. It may not be good leadership according to today's standards and the rationale might even rub against a purely organizational view of the church, but because it's God's plan and from God, it accomplishes his purpose.

God describes the character traits of those he wants to lead his church. These qualities are evidence of God living within. They are the result of new birth and the presence of the Holy Spirit and are evidenced by a spiritual life filled by God. They reveal that these leaders have been humbled before God and have experienced renewal of mind and conformation to the image of Christ. By describing these qualities, God places an emphasis on who a person is over what a person does or how a person leads. This truth is particularly evident in the following two passages.

> An elder must be a man whose life cannot be spoken against. He must be faithful to his wife. He must exhibit self-control, live wisely, and have a good reputation. He must enjoy having guests in his home and must be able to teach. He must not be a heavy drinker or be violent. He must be gentle, peace loving, and not one who loves money. He must manage his own family well, with children who respect and obey him. (1 Tim. 3:2–4 NLT)

> An elder must be well thought of for his good life. He must be faithful to his wife, and his children must be believers who are not wild or rebellious. An elder must live a blameless life because he is God's minister. He must not be arrogant or quick-tempered; he must not be a heavy drinker, violent, or greedy for money. He must enjoy having guests in his home and must love all that is good. He must live wisely and be fair. He must live a devout and disciplined life. He must have a strong and steadfast belief in the trustworthy message he was taught; then he will be able to encourage others with right teaching and show those who oppose it where they are wrong. (Titus 1:6–9 NLT)

Fundamentally, the Word of God underscores *character* over skills, talents, or spiritual gifting when it comes to defining a spiritual leader.

THE INFLUENCE OF A BIBLICAL LEADER

Hebrews 13:7 says, "Remember your leaders, who spoke the word of God to you. Consider the outcome of their way of life and imitate their faith." This injunction supports the teaching throughout the Bible that godly leaders provide a picture of the Christian life for others to follow.

Obedience to the Word of God is what sets spiritual leaders apart from other types of leaders. These leaders are not only knowledgeable, but are men and women who are being transformed by the Word of God. Their lives demonstrate the practice of the presence of God.

These leaders have journeyed down the road of life long enough that the evidence of obedience is seen by all: Belief has become sight, righteous behavior has brought maturity and grace, which leads to personal transformation, and has positively influenced others. Their marriages have matured into rare and beautiful portraits of love. Their children have followed in the steps of faith. Their careers have demonstrated the value of people formation, not just monetary rewards.

What happens when leaders fail? Leaders are not perfect, but they of all people should be transparent! They should be honest in confessing their sins and seeking proper resolutions and restitution for personal failures. Keeping accountable to God and his people typically guards anyone, leaders included, against the major disasters of life.

A SPIRIT-FILLED LEADER

As we have already noted, Paul commands biblical leaders to be filled by the Holy Spirit. What does this mean? According to Ephesians 5:18–20, to be filled by the Holy Spirit means that one is not controlled by any external or internal force other than the Spirit of God. The person of the Holy Spirit living in us produces the motivation for our behavior, decisions, and communication. Ephesians 5:19–20 indicates that proper worship provides the context for the working of the Holy Spirit in and through the Christian leader. Colossians 3:16 supplements this teaching with a parallel focus on allowing the Word of Christ to live within us.

Therefore, to be filled by the Holy Spirit means we yield to his control (Holy Spirit) and guidance (Word of Christ) moment by moment. This process requires that we as believers humble ourselves before God, yielding to him the control of our minds, emotions, and wills. As a Christian learns this walk with Christ, he or she will be conformed to God's image and become qualified to serve as a leader in his church.

Acts 11:1–4 illustrates a proper response by the apostle Peter to criticism for his ministry to Cornelius and his household. Some of the Jewish believers in Jerusalem, when they heard that Peter had entered a Gentile's home and eaten with him, were critical of this behavior because it violated the Jewish customs and laws. Instead of defending himself or arguing with them, Peter "explained everything to them precisely as it had happened" (Acts 11:4). As Peter's response shows us, Spirit-filled leaders are not defensive. This nondefensiveness builds confidence and safety in those they lead. Safe leaders obtain better information in any situation. Because the leader is safe, people are willing to be open and honest. Safe leaders gain discernment from this information and are better equipped to make wise biblical decisions. The Holy Spirit's control transforms disciples into spiritual leaders.

THE DEVOTION OF A BIBLICAL LEADER

Biblical leaders are devoted to pursuing God. Spiritual leaders seek God, trust God, and live for God (Ps. 27:4; Prov. 3:5–6; Gal. 2:20). However, with the demands of performance that leaders keenly feel, the "God question" is not always addressed. Much of this book attempts to show how leaders can answer the God question. That is, "Do I actively trust God in all areas of my life and ministry?" Easier said than done.

We see biblical leadership as an active and dynamic relationship with God and his people. Therefore, at the core of our lives is the essential need to be loved by God. Godly leaders have been melted and molded by his grace, not by our competency. Though structure and form characterize all healthy organizations, the supreme ingredient in all relationships is love.

And the first place love needs to be experienced is in the life of the leader. Loveless leaders seek to use others, not love them. Without love, the Bible says, we are just making a lot of noise. In other words, a leader without love is "just blowing smoke."

While sitting in a hotel in St. Petersburg, Russia, I (Tim) reflected on a question asked by one of the older pastors in the city. We were discussing the possibilities of churches doing ministry together with Luis Palau for a season of evangelism. He inquired, "Does Luis Palau love the Russian people?" More than vision, organizational structure, goals, money, or impact in his city, this seasoned pastor demanded to know, "Do you love us?"

Love is the glue that binds people together in dynamic relationship and holy service for God. Churches are healed and become healthy when love empowers the leaders' relationships.

How Are Biblical Leaders Chosen?

The biblical answer is clear. Leaders are discovered in the context of relationships. Leaders will arise as the church lives together and serves our Lord. As we "do life," godly leaders become evident to all. As the church focuses on the teaching of God's Word, worship, sharing the good news, and serving one another, leaders will surface. Leaders are not to be selected because of their gifts alone, but rather because of their character.

They are to be Christlike.

The challenge for us as a church today is the void of relationships. We live in a fractured world where relationships have become secondary to personal goals and ambitions. The affluence in America has widened the door for independent living. So rather than choosing to invest our lives in relationships, we have chosen to travel, move, recreate, become workaholics, obtain more education, etc. Taken within the context of life's totality, these things are not bad. But in a church setting, they can be disastrous because they often become substitutes for significant and meaningful relation-ships with others.

Community is a term we use for a geographical boundary or a cen-ter for recreation. It is most often used to describe a location rather than to describe the relationships within a group of people learning to live life together. But it is in the context of this kind of community that relationships are formed, which make it possible to identify truly Spirit-filled leaders.

How can healing and health come to the thousands of churches who are suffering from a terminal condition? Spirit-filled leaders are a critical "antidote" to this condition. Spirit-filled leaders must be affirmed and chosen on the basis of biblical instruction. And we identify these leaders best in the context of a living community. These leaders, when walking in the power of the Holy Spirit, will be ready to embark on a journey of healing, health, and holy impact in their communities.

PART TWO

PRINCIPLES OF SPIRIT-LED LEADERSHIP AND MANAGEMENT

CHAPTER 5

HEARING GOD

When my (Allen) children were young, they were endowed with amazing hearing. Mary and I called it selective hearing—keenly selective hearing. One day, as I was going out the door to work, I said to one of them, "Please clean your bedroom today." That was a simple enough request and I said it loud enough. And considering we were in the same room, it should have been easily understood. Yet that evening the bedroom was a mess.

Assuming the best, I inquired, "What is going on? I asked you to clean your room."

"I didn't hear you ask me to do that!" was the quick response.

Another time with no children around, I might quietly say to my wife, Mary, "Would you like an ice cream cone?"

The child, who claimed to be unable to hear me while in the same room, would come from some other part of the house and ask, "Hey, great idea. Can we all go and get ice cream?"

Is it possible that God's children could develop the same selective hearing?

Jeremiah says so. "To whom can I speak and give warning? Who will listen to me? Their ears are closed so they cannot hear. The word of the LORD is offensive to them; they find no pleasure in it" (Jer. 6:10).

Again he says, "But they did not listen or pay attention; instead, they followed the stubborn inclinations of their evil hearts" (Jer. 7:24).

Jeremiah throws the tension of our selective hearing right in the faces of God's children today. To whom will we listen? For a moment, think about times we have thought, said, or done something that in our hearts we knew God would not be pleased about. Whose voice were we paying attention to at the time? The subject of hearing God is a huge issue today. It was a huge issue in the early church. Notice Peter's warning to his readers:

> We did not follow cleverly invented stories when we told you about the power and coming of our Lord Jesus Christ, but we were eyewitnesses of his majesty. For he received honor and glory from God the Father when the voice came to him from the Majestic Glory, saying, "This is my Son, whom I love; with him I am well pleased." We ourselves heard this voice that came from heaven when we were with him on the sacred mountain.
>
> And we have the word of the prophets made more certain, and you will do well to pay attention to it, as to a light shining in a dark place, until the day dawns and the morning star rises in your hearts. (2 Peter 1:16–19)

The disciples heard God as a voice from heaven and from the prophets in the written Word. Peter cautions us to pay attention to the Word as we would a light in places where it is dark.

Have you ever been walking on a treacherous path at night with a flashlight? In that situation, we rely on the light to assure we are walking on the path. What is the flashlight for? To show us the way.

How do you hear God? Many books have been written on this subject—some extremely helpful. The best books on the subject list the sources of input as the Bible, the counsel of trusted people, our circumstances, and our minds.

THE BIBLE

Back in the midseventies, because of God's specific answer to prayer, I (Allen) was face-to-face with a man, now deceased, who walked with and loved deeply the person of Jesus Christ. The purpose of my meeting with him was to ask how he knew so clearly what it was God wanted him to do, even moment by moment throughout the day.

His answer was profound. Rather than go into a story about how to hear God, he asked me two questions, then based on my response, asked me a third question. Here are his questions:

1. "Is there anything written in the Bible that you do not believe based on how you react to life, your emotions in difficult situations, your fears about the future, your priorities, and in general how you live life?"
2. "Are there any commandments, directives, or teachings in the Bible that you are not now obeying?"

I had to respond yes to both questions. Without even going into the details of my yes answer, he asked a third question:

3. "If your faith in and your love [affection] for Christ is so shallow that you cannot walk in the light he has clearly given you [believe and obey], how can you expect that you would believe and obey him if you knew more?"

To make matters worse, I had to admit to him that I had never even read the entire Bible.

He went on. "Allen, God has given you a love letter, providing you the opportunity to get to know him, his passions, his desire for you to love him in return, and how your love for him will play out through your obedience and faith. You are making this too complicated. It is about a love relationship and you already have most of what you need to live in a love relationship with him. You have it in the Bible. I suggest you get familiar with it. I believe that when the day comes that you need more insight, God will provide it. Remember, you have within you the mind of Christ right now."

COUNSEL

Some say that we can hear from God through the providential counsel of trusted, mature people. It is harder to place confidence in people than in the Bible. There have been many individuals who we thought we could trust but later failed us. However, rather than throwing out all counsel, perhaps it would be better to recognize that, though this advice can be good, unlike the Bible it is not perfectly reliable. We believe that Scripture should remain the foundation of God's revelation to us, with counsel remaining a source of confirmation of what we believe is God's leading.

CIRCUMSTANCES

Many believe that circumstances can be a clue to God's leading. The problem with circumstances as a source of God's leading is that our interpretation of our circumstances may be clouded. It is easy to miss the influence of the flesh or the Evil One in a situation that is pleasant to us. Through the centuries, God has often placed his saints in circumstances of stress. It is equally difficult to see God's leading while going through disaster. It is likely that we could misinterpret our circumstances and, therefore, what God is communicating to us. Similar to counsel, our interpretation of our circumstances as a source of confirmation about God's leading is not perfectly reliable. We must ask God to help us see him in our circumstances.

GOD'S SPIRIT AND OUR MINDS

In 1 Corinthians, Paul tells us that God reveals what he has prepared for us and that he does it through his Spirit.

> However, as it is written:
>> "No eye has seen,
>> no ear has heard,
>> no mind has conceived
>> what God has prepared for those who love him"—
>
> but God has revealed it to us by his Spirit. The Spirit searches all things, even the deep things of God. (1 Cor. 2:9–10)

Paul also tells us that God not only reveals himself to us by his Spirit, but that he has put his Spirit in us so we are able to understand what God has given us.

Paul continues by stating how a person who does not know God cannot understand the things of God, and then he finishes this thought by quoting Isaiah 40:13.

> We have not received the spirit of the world but the Spirit who is from God, that we may understand what God has freely given us. This is what we speak, not in words taught us by human wisdom but in words taught by the Spirit, expressing spiritual truths in spiritual words. The man without the Spirit does not accept the things that come from the Spirit of God, for they are foolishness to him, and he cannot understand them, because they are spiritually discerned. The spiritual man makes judgments about all things, but he himself is not subject to any man's judgment:
> "For who has known the mind of the Lord that he may instruct him?" But we have the mind of Christ. (1 Cor. 2:12–16)

The Bible is clear; with God's Spirit in us, we do have the mind of Christ in us, and it is God's intent to do a work in our minds.

> Do not conform any longer to the pattern of this world, but be transformed by the renewing of your mind. Then you will be able to test and approve what God's will is—his good, pleasing and perfect will. (Rom. 12:2)

BARRIERS TO HEARING GOD

It may be helpful at this point to look at what gets in the way of hearing God—whether from Scripture, counsel, circumstances, or our minds.

Time to Listen

Who has time to listen these days? Life is going from one "to do" to another. We have a living to earn. We have a home to maintain. We have our church activities. We have children. There are the favorite television programs to watch or movies to see or games to attend.

Life is hectic today. We have convinced ourselves that we do not have enough time, and listening suffers.

Real listening is love because love focuses on the other person. Love takes communication; communication takes time. A father once said to his pastor, "I may not give my children much time, but what time I give is quality time." The pastor said, "Baloney, there is no such thing as planned quality time with anyone. The quality of the time is in the hands of the other person, not just you. It takes much time invested to have quality time with someone." Hearing someone with an understanding ear (quality hearing) takes time.

Hearing God is similar; it requires time for listening with an ear ready to listen.

The Tempo of Life

When Jesus Christ walked on earth, he walked two to three miles per hour. While he was walking, he was talking and teaching. He spent hours of the day conversing with his Father. Life was slower then—no more carefree, but slower.

The tempo of life may seem similar to "lack of time," but the difference lies in what is crammed into any one hour.

Television is one of the industrialized world's primary places of relaxation and entertainment. Some homes have several televisions so family members can watch programs of their choice. However, have you ever watched a television screen when it was too far away for you to be involved with the program? Did you notice how rapidly scenes change? You could measure scenes in seconds, and even then you would probably not find many that last ten seconds. While the scenes scream past our eyes, the tempo of the music, the words, and the sound effects hammer at us. This is anything BUT relaxing. Professionals design the programming to grip your attention. The rapid-fire pace does a lot to destroy an atmosphere for meaningful listening.

The nearly instant communication of telephone and e-mail make it possible for us to perform far more of whatever we think we need to perform per hour, but at a great cost. Our hectic technology-based communication has replaced much of the face-to-face communication. It is easy to see why there is a drought today in real hearing.

Real hearing is hearing between the words. We might say that real hearing is hearing with the third ear, and the third ear hears better face-to-face.

The Desires of Our Hearts (Our Affections)

The lack of time and the tempo of our lives muffles our ability to hear (listen to) God or hear (listen to) other people. However, limited time and rapid tempo may not be as significant a barrier to hearing as we would like to believe. It may be the issue is more that we simply choose not to listen. Remaining silent before God or with another person is uncomfortable.

Most people want to talk. They do not want to listen. Why? Perhaps it is because when we talk we feel in control or important. Even in time with God, believers monopolize the time by talking. In these cases, prayer (a visit with God) is mostly asking God for something. We pray for God to make us (or someone else) healthy, to provide what we need and want, to make us a better people, or to help someone else see that he is wrong and we are right or whatever else.

It seems that this kind of life is more about receiving love than loving, more about talking than listening, more about getting than giving.

We will make the time for what is most important to us. Spending time with family or God may be important to us; however, the urgent things that may not be important in the end seem to loom over our heads and take over our time with family or God. Simply stated, it is more important to us to get rid of urgent things than to take care of important but not urgent things. It is usually our choice—whether we recognize it or not.

It is what we value, the center of our affections, that controls our behavior and choices. When we are the center of our affections, then listening to others will be a priority only when what they have to say will affect us—when there is something important for us to gain or lose. Perhaps at times we listen to make a good impression or so we will not be embarrassed when it is our turn to say something. We are still the center of our listening.

The Focus of Our Love

In chapter 3, we read that God's desire for our love is his priority for us. The time necessary to love God is no different than it is with a family member or friend. Time alone with our Lord with a listening heart is critical to hear him and to grow in our love for him. Time spent reading his love letter to us will give us understanding about his sovereignty and the depth of his love for us.

Many people believe that a disciplined reading of the Bible coupled with disciplined prayer will result in God loving us more, or at least looking favorably on us. Please dispel that thought. God will not love us any greater because of our great discipline of Bible reading and prayer. God loves us infinitely now. However, we should find that because of our disciplined time with God (pouring over his love letter to us while praying and listening) we grow in our love for Jesus Christ and an awareness of what pleases or displeases him.

Dr. Ronald Frost, a professor at Multnomah Biblical Seminary, captures this relationship of time with God and hearing him. Dr. Frost shares the story of when he was a boy. His father did not have a printed rule book, but he knew his father well from the years of close interaction with him. Dr. Frost knew all through the day whether his actions or attitudes would be pleasing or displeasing to his father because he knew his father well. He knew his father well because he had spent time with him.

As we meet with churches having problems, we find that many of the leaders spend little time with God either in conversation (talking and listening prayer) or in reading his love letter—the letter he has provided them to get to know him.

Think about a young couple when they begin to discover that they are mutually interested in each other. What do they do? They spend every available moment with each other sharing about themselves, listening to each other's dreams, fears, experiences, and values. When they are apart and receive a letter from the other, they read the letter repeatedly. When they are reading, they feel closer to the one they love.

Our growing relationship with God should be the same way.

Since it is God's number one commandment for us to love him with all our heart, all our soul, and our entire mind, it would seem that it would be important to us as leaders to do just that. To love God with our entire heart, soul, and mind requires that we spend focused time with him in order to know and love him deeply. And hearing God corresponds directly with knowing and loving him. No matter how we look at it, our lives as believers or leaders pivot around taking time to know and love our sovereign and loving Jesus Christ.

Reading the Bible is reading God's love letter to us, so that we might get to know him well and fall more deeply in love with him. If we wrote a love letter to someone we loved, we would hope they would not read our letter out of a sense of duty and discipline. Instead, we would hope they would embrace every word because they love us and want to know us better and in some way grow closer to us.

Idols in the Heart

When the leaders of Israel went to Ezekiel wanting a word from God (Ezek. 14), God responded by pointing out that these leaders had idols in their hearts and "stumbling blocks" before their faces and that God would deal with them in accordance with those issues. Obviously, God knew that they did not ask for a word from him with the intent to receive the word in their hearts and take appropriate response. These double-minded men were interested in their own power, respect, recognition, approval, safety, and comfort. Each was his own biggest idol. They loved themselves, giving lip service to their relationship to God.

This is still happening today among many church leaders. As church leaders or as individuals, we may be going to God asking for a word about his will, yet keeping the right to make the final decision. Other things have to be considered, things that tug at our hearts. If those other things keep us from responding to what we know God is calling us to, these things are idols.

Those idols are things that society has convinced people are essential for life. The idol may be a house that is bigger or more expensive than Jesus would have had us buy if we had let him decide. Of course, it could go the other way. The house we have may be smaller or less expensive than Jesus would have had us buy, perhaps for a larger ministry to which he may have been calling us. Other idols may be success, power, recognition, respect, approval, predictability, comfort, or any number of other things.

Like the leaders of Israel, we can wrap all these idols into one—
"the self." People tend to be their own biggest idols. We can easily lull
ourselves into the illusion that God is pleased with how we live,
because after all, we make good money and we give to the church.
Look how much we do for God. God wants us to be happy and enjoy
life, does he not?

As a church leadership team, we may use words that tell people
we are inquiring about God's will, yet keep in our hearts the right to
make the final decision. Or we may hold a subtle yet real expectation
that God's answer would only be within our preconceived limits. It is
possible that a church could turn a church ministry into an idol. It may
not even occur to us that God might have something different for the
church from the direction we have been going.

Remember the carousel when you were a kid? It was a lot of fun
when you were small, but after awhile it probably occurred to you
that you weren't going anywhere—just around and around. In the
movies, the horse and rider always went places, so you wanted to
move up to the real thing. Yet when the time came to make that
switch, perhaps at the beach or summer camp, it was scary getting up
on that horse for the first time. Oh, the exhilaration when you did it—
you rode the horse and actually went somewhere.

Life and ministry in our churches can be much like that carousel.
We feel like we have been riding the carousel horses up and down and
round and round. But God wants us to exchange the imitation horse
for a real one and to ride off with him to an adventure full of risk and
uncertainty, yet with him fully at our side. It can be scary when our
churches start looking at getting up on that horse. That fear can act like
an idol that controls us.

Competing Noises

Some years ago, an artist was explaining his view of impression-
ism. He was trying to explain the difference between painting what
the camera sees and what the mind sees. To explain the difference, he

asked his listeners to look at Mount Rainier, which was in view, and notice how big it was. He then showed a picture of roughly the same scene. Mount Rainier was only a small part of the picture. The artist explained that the mind is able to filter the total view received by the eye and to focus attention on only a small part of what it sees.

We hear in much the same way. Have you noticed how when we are in a social situation, such as a restaurant or party, with people milling around visiting, music playing in the background, plates and glasses clanking, everyone talking and laughing, we are still able to have a discussion with one person? We seem to be able to sort out what that person is saying from all the sounds that are coming at us. Our minds are able to filter out sounds that are not pertinent at the time.

Even more amazing is that in the middle of that noise, including the voice of the person we are listening to, we are able to hear our son or daughter off in the near distance crying out, "Mommy, Daddy, where are you?" Is it not amazing how out of all that clamor, our child's voice grabs our attention—not someone else's child, just ours? Why is that? It is because we know that voice intimately. With love, we have spent a great deal of time listening to that voice. Through our relationship with our child, we have an intense interest in hearing that voice.

Jesus said, "My sheep recognize my voice; I know them, and they follow me" (John 10:27 NLT). That brings us back to the need to be in a dependent love relationship with Jesus Christ—to know the voice of the One who loves us most in order to filter out the competing noises.

EXPECTATION TO HEAR GOD

There are two factors that determine what we expect to hear from God: our view of our ability to hear and our view of who God is.

In his book *Christ Is All*, David Bryant addresses the believer's tendency to spontaneously talk or not talk about Jesus Christ. He says the following:

> What if He [Jesus] usually seems to be indifferent to secur-
> ing meaningful solutions for the struggles of our lives?
> What if He comes across to us as offering little immediate
> hope for broken relationships, or financially besieged fam-
> ilies, or bungled battles with addictions, or our beaten-up
> sense of self-worth, or the breathless bustling of our
> churchly activities, or the moral bankruptcy of our commu-
> nities? What if the Jesus we call Lord is perceived
> frequently as incapably involved with us when we are
> drowning in dark moments of despair? Why would we
> want to make him a major topic of conversation when we
> gather together?[1]

If Bryant paints a word picture similar to our real view of God, then why would we expect to hear from God? Or for that matter, why would we want to hear from him?

Many believers today do not expect to hear God because they do not understand that they can hear God. That idea just does not reconcile with the rational thinking of the Western world.

HOW DO WE HEAR FROM GOD?

As we have already discussed, the most obvious place to start is Scripture—the Bible. Be careful, because there is a question that we need to answer first: "Do we really want to hear from God?"

Many believers say they want to hear God's voice—they even pray about it. Yet look how much God has already spoken to his children through his Word. Perhaps believers should be more consistently obedient to the Word they have already heard.

Paul wrote, "Therefore, I urge you, brothers, in view of God's mercy, to offer your bodies as living sacrifices, holy and pleasing to God—this is your spiritual act of worship. Do not conform any longer to the pattern of this world, but be transformed by the renewing of your mind. Then you will be able to test and approve what God's will is—his good, pleasing and perfect will" (Rom. 12:1–2).

Bring this verse to its logical conclusion and it has to affect myriad choices we make. What house will we buy, and what will be our criteria if we are a living sacrifice, holy (set apart) and pleasing to God? If we are a living sacrifice, what movies will we watch or what discussions will we not enter into? If we are a living sacrifice, how will we treat a difficult person at church—the one we want to avoid?

Ezekiel 14 suggests that our hearing of God may be linked to our affections—in direct proportion to the idols or lack of idols in our hearts.

We have come to believe the number one controlling factor in hearing God is our relationship with him, knowing and loving him. If we want to know more about God's will for us, we have to start by getting to know God more. We have to open our Bibles and start reading his love letter, not to get some verse that we can quote or use, but to know better the God of the Bible. Spend more time with him, just as we would someone we were courting. Talk to him more in prayer, tell him how much we love him, and bask in his love for us. Occasionally, be silent and meditate before him. Let our minds dwell on him. Ask him to help us recognize doors he is opening or closing. Do all this with him alone and together as a leadership team. Please do not turn this into an obligation.

God already loves us infinitely. The time we spend with him will not cause him to love us more; but it may have an enormous impact on our love for him, and as a result, our love for others and our ability to hear him.

It is critical for us as leaders and as leadership teams to allow God to lead us. Therefore, it is critical that we are intentionally and continuously crucifying idols and drawing closer to him into a deeper and deeper love relationship.

CHAPTER 6

LOVING PEOPLE, NOT USING PEOPLE

D uring my time of education and for years into my banking career, I (Allen) learned about a number of concepts regarding leadership and management. One of those concepts had to do with "input factors." Simplistically, input factors are what you invest into a process that results in output. People use the term *input factor* in a variety of disciplines, but I became familiar with it as it is primarily used in business.

As best that I recall, the primary input factors in business are money, real and personal property, and people (usually referred to by the impersonal term, human resources). It never was particularly exciting to me to know that I was a human resource. I never did feel like one; I always felt like a person. For as long as I can remember, in banking and in most of the companies large enough to have departments, the group that was responsible for people was called the Human Resource Department, or HR for short.

As far as employer/employee correspondence is concerned, I never did get a letter from the bank that said, "Dear Human Resource." The worst I ever received was "Dear Valued Employee." I have to admit that "Dear Valued Employee" was still better than "Dear Human Resource." It could have been worse. The letter could have said, "To whom it may concern." Fortunately, most letters said, "Dear Allen."

When I left banking and went to seminary, I said good-bye to Human Resources. I thought that in ministry, both churches and parachurch ministries, they must have something other than Human Resources; they must have something like the Ministry Care Department, or maybe the Servant Service Section.

To my dismay, even in large churches and in many parachurch ministries, some still use the term *human resource,* though many use the term *Personnel Department.* I like that better; I am still a person.

By now you are asking, "Where is this guy going?" In this chapter, we will be addressing a tendency in churches and parachurch ministries to forget how important people are to God. We will be looking at the struggle leadership has, often unknowingly, of using people rather than loving people. We will be examining how a leader executes time management through delegation and training in the new light of ministry.

THE LEADER IS THE SLAVE

To me, one of the most powerful stories in Scripture is in John 13. Jesus and his disciples were eating a meal when Jesus got up and began washing their feet. What makes this act difficult to grasp is that, in a home that had servants at that time, washing the feet of the guests was the job of the servant lowest in the order of hierarchy. Jesus was assuming the role of the lowest servant. After he finished serving them, he taught them.

"You call me 'Teacher' and 'Lord,' and rightly so, for that is what I am. Now that I, your Lord and Teacher, have washed your feet, you also should wash one another's feet. I have set you an example that you should do as I have done for you" (John 13:13–15).

For a long time, I believed that the foot-washing lesson was for leaders to remember that they are serving those they lead. I think that is where they get the term *servant-leader.* Lately, I discovered an additional lesson I believe Jesus wanted us to learn; it has to do with the role Jesus accepted as being the lowest of servants.

At the beginning of John 13, it says that Jesus knew that it was time for him to go back to the Father. Jesus knew that he was about to return to the glory he came from, that of God himself. Yet he took this lowest of all positions. From a worldly point of view, you could draw a continuum line with God at one end and the lowest person in the world at the other end. Jesus is obviously at God's end of the continuum. But Jesus demonstrated an extreme shift by taking the servant role at the very opposite end of the continuum. And Jesus did not give up his position as Christ while he made that shift. That is the power of this story.

The lesson that Jesus demonstrated was that leaders always have two roles. First, the leader is a steward or agent for Christ, leading as Christ's representative. The leader is not more important or valuable than any other follower of Christ.

Second, the leader is a servant, serving those being led and doing it from the *heart*. This means that the leader leads while serving those being led. If the leader does not make the switch in his heart, but only in his behavior, he could easy become like the Pharisees. Jesus is asking leaders to do what he did, which is to accept these two roles. We will identify a leader who accepts both of these roles as a servant-leader.

The two roles of servant leadership are seen clearly in the Great Commandment, found in Matthew 22. The leader is to love God, which is foundational to the stewardship role of leading the people of Christ's church. The leader is to love others, which is foundational to the role of serving others (those led).

USING PEOPLE

In our travels and meetings with a variety of church leaders, we have noticed a tendency for ministry leaders to perceive people as "human resources" and to forget their role as ministers to those people. When people become only a "human resource," an "input factor" invested to produce a successful output, they become a tool for leaders to use for their desired result. We believe the vast majority of Christian leaders do not intentionally ponder how they might use people for their own purposes or to make themselves look good or make their work easier. We believe that the tendency to use people (to see them as primarily a human resource) is a function of several influences:

- Using people can be a result of forgetting (or ignorance of) the depth of the stewardship role to which Christ called his leaders.
- Using people can be a result of forgetting (or ignorance of) the depth of the servant leadership role to which Christ called his leaders.
- Using people can often stem from the current trend of adopting secular leadership and management techniques without overlaying them with God's love-based model of servant leadership.
- Using people can result from a lack of awareness about the impact that normal leadership and management activities have on people without the influence of love through servant leadership. *We are not arguing against the use of leadership and management techniques, only their use without overlaying God's love for his children.*

For the rest of this chapter, we will be focusing on the role of servant leadership to minister to the people being led. In later chapters, we will explore the servant-leader's role as a steward for God. This stewardship relates to leading the church toward its God-given purpose and mission through God's unique vision and plan for the ministry.

MINISTRY OF DELEGATION

One of the significant activities of a leader is assigning and directing the activities of those he leads, an activity frequently called delegation.

A leaders usually delegates for one of two reasons:

1. Delegation to get something done or save the leader time.

2. Delegation to accomplish God's purpose and mission for the church while at the same time providing a means to serve, love, and develop the servant.

1. Delegation for the Sole Purpose of Getting Something Done or Saving the Leader Time

Jack was pastor over the children's ministries and had been so for sixteen years. He was fortunate to have a number of very good teachers, most of whom required little oversight. It was that time of year again when Jack had to line up teachers for the season from September through May, and he was busy at it. All the classes now had teachers except for third-grade girls.

Maggie had been teaching that group of girls now for nine years and was fantastic. It was a large group, but Maggie had a real gift at recruiting volunteers to help her, even when she was going to be absent herself. She was very organized, an excellent communicator, well liked, and respected. Yet she had a desire to move on to something more challenging.

Most teachers did not have an assistant and so had to do everything themselves unless they could find someone to help. However, Janet was Maggie's assistant. She started helping Maggie while she was a senior in high school. With Maggie's coaching and encouragement, she could step in when Maggie was away and the class functioned normally. Janet was looking forward to taking over the class on her own. However, Pastor Jack needed them to stay together with the same class again. So they agreed.

What is notable about this scenario is that Jack needed someone to handle the third-grade girls, and that is what he got. From Jack's perspective, he got the job done, and all is well because, after all, Maggie and Janet enjoy what they do.

Joyce was the women's ministry director over a large group of three hundred women. She enjoyed this ministry. Then again, she enjoyed most everything in life, including her tennis club. She would do more in the tennis club if she had the time, but she did not. Women's ministry consumed too much time.

It occurred to Joyce that one of the things she did that took much time was the word processing, printing, and mailing of the monthly women's ministry newsletter. It had grown to a six-page document and required about five hours a week to produce.

One of the women in the group was Naomi, an older woman but retired from being a secretary for a publishing company. Naomi was so good that she could do the newsletter in her sleep. The problem was that Naomi was tired of word processing and publishing and wanted to take some Bible courses to prepare her to spend her later years as a missionary in Latin America. She just needed more Bible training.

Joyce really needed Naomi to take over the newsletter so Joyce could become more involved in the tennis club. What was Naomi going to say? She felt guilty for thinking about herself and not Joyce's need. So she agreed.

Joyce accomplished her goal. She was able to recover the five hours a week she wanted in order to do something else. How is Naomi? She is doing an unbelievable job at the newsletter. It is amazingly professional, just as Joyce had expected.

Both Jack and Joyce accomplished what they wanted to accomplish. Both Jack and Joyce led people to accomplish the ministry they believe God called them to lead. Jack filled all the teacher roles he wanted to fill, including the third-grade girls' class by keeping Maggie and Janet. He had a great team to get the job done, and done well. Joyce accomplished what she wanted to accomplish. She now has gifted Naomi putting out a newsletter that any women's director would covet.

But what about God's vision for Maggie, Janet, and Naomi? Maggie is still doing third-grade girls, even though she is challenged to step into something more stretching. Janet is not having the opportunity to try her wings as she would like to do and feels she is ready for. Naomi is doing a great job, but the ministry to which God has called her will have to wait.

THE SERVANT-LEADER APPROACH

Let us run those two scenarios again, only this time let us change the motivations of both Pastor Jack and Joyce to be that of the servant-leader who is a lover of those he is leading. Remember the two roles of the servant-leader: (1) to be a steward or agent for Christ, leading as Christ's representative, and (2) to be a servant, serving those being led.

2. Delegation to Accomplishing God's Purpose and Mission for the Church While at the Same Time Providing a Means to Serve, Love, and Develop the Servant

Jack was pastor over the children's ministries and had been so for sixteen years. He was fortunate to have a number of very good teachers, most of whom required little oversight. It was that time of year again when Jack had to line up teachers for the season from September through May and he was busy at it. All the classes now had teachers except for third-grade girls.

Maggie had been teaching that group of girls now for nine years and was fantastic. It was a large group, but Maggie had a real gift at recruiting volunteers to help her, even when she was going to be absent herself. She was very organized, an excellent communicator, well liked, and respected. However, she had a desire to move on to something more challenging.

Most teachers did not have an assistant and so had to do everything themselves, unless they could find someone to help. However, Janet was Maggie's assistant. She started helping Maggie while she was a senior in high school. With Maggie's coaching and encouragement, she could step in when Maggie was away and the class functioned normally. Janet was looking forward to taking over the class on her own.

Maggie and Janet were a great team. Pastor Jack would love to have them stay together with the same class again—it would mean less work for him, but it was not the best for the future of Maggie or Janet.

Maggie had a gift for organization and leadership. She recognized new talent when she saw it and knew how to develop it. The gift God had given Maggie was something this church could use; for that matter, any church could use it. Asking Maggie to teach the third-grade girls was no longer a growing experience for her and would limit what God may want to do in her life for the years to come.

Janet was young, but was fully able to handle her own class and wanted to.

Jack pondered what he could do to give Maggie a stretching, growing experience and still accomplish what was needed to be consistent with the church's purpose and mission for God in the lives of the children.

It did not take long for Jack to realize he could minister to these two servants while at the same time perform his role as a ministry leader. He asked Janet to step up and take the lead teacher role for the third-grade girls. Janet was thrilled to have Pastor Jack trust her with the challenge. Maggie had trained Janet well, and Janet was ready for the stretch.

Jack then asked Maggie if she would be willing to be his assistant. This would accomplish two things. Maggie could start a new challenge with all the new experiences it would bring, and Jack could begin developing his replacement, so he could consider any new challenge God may put in front of him.

What a deal. Jack was a dual-role servant-leader. He acted as a steward of the responsibilities God gave him regarding the purpose, mission, and unique vision of the church. At the same time, he was a steward of the responsibilities God gave him regarding serving, loving, and discipling two of God's servants.

᠅

Joyce was the women's ministry director over a large group of three hundred women. She enjoyed this ministry. Then again, she enjoyed most everything in life, including her tennis club. Joyce saw the tennis club as an outreach opportunity to women. Establishing a new outreach like that was just what the women's ministry needed to spur on more women to do something similar. However, it was impossible since the women's ministry consumed so much of her time.

It occurred to Joyce that one of the things she did that took much time was the word processing, printing, and mailing of the monthly women's ministry newsletter. It had grown to a six-page document and required about five hours a week to produce. If Joyce could delegate that to someone else, it would free the time for Joyce to focus on developing more outreach; something in line with the purpose and mission of the church.

One of the women in the group was Naomi, an older woman and retired from being a secretary for a publishing company. Naomi was so good that she could do the newsletter in her sleep. The problem was that Naomi was tired of typing and publishing and wanted to take some Bible courses to prepare her to spend her later years as a missionary in Latin America. Naomi spoke Spanish well, but she just needed more Bible training.

What was Joyce to do?

Joyce realized that since Naomi was retired, she had time to do the newsletter and take an online Bible course. And Joyce could be her mentor. In addition, Joyce thought that Naomi, as she was ready, could begin to write a women's Bible course that could be published in the newsletter.

Naomi was thrilled. What a challenge. Not only did she have a great mentor and friend in Joyce, she had the opportunity to learn two things. She learned more Bible, which was something she needed on the mission field. She also learned how to write Bible lessons for women, something she also needed on the mission field. Joyce now had the time to begin leading a new thrust in women's ministry.

Joyce was a servant-leader for God, leading people to accomplish Christ's purpose, mission, and unique vision for the church. At the same time she helped accomplish Christ's purpose, mission, and unique vision for Naomi through serving, loving, and discipling her.

IMPLICATIONS

In the second scenario, Jack and Joyce were able to see people as more than a human resource to use to accomplish ministry. They saw ministry as an opportunity to accomplish God's purpose, mission, and unique vision for the church while simultaneously accomplishing God's purpose, mission, and unique vision in the lives of the ministers.

GETTING TO KNOW PEOPLE

Another significant activity of servant-leaders, besides delegating, is getting to know each person being led. To know someone is one of the most difficult yet awesome tasks a leader faces. Yet it is the key to maintaining a balance between leading God's people to accomplish the purpose, mission, and unique vision of the church, while serving the lives of the ministers.

To know someone who is under our leadership is difficult because it requires a great deal of us.

- It requires listening with the "third ear." That ear hears what the heart is saying.
- It requires selecting carefully the questions to be asked. Not all questions are appropriate. There are some areas of a person's life that are not anyone's business but God's or certain special and trusted people.
- It requires trustworthiness at all times, which means keeping everything that is said confidential unless there

is permission to repeat it. Being trustworthy also requires
a guarding of intentions. It is easy to fall into the trap of
asking questions that can later be used as weapons to
manipulate a person.

- Listening, asking questions, and trustworthiness require
us as leaders to be sure we have no hidden agendas.

Both Jack and Joyce had to spend time getting to know Maggie,
Janet, and Naomi. They had to learn the same information we have to
learn about those under our direct leadership. What are their hopes,
dreams, and fears? How long have they been doing what it is they are
doing? Is it time to start challenging them again? What gift has God
given them? What training do they need? We will come up with much
more to learn as we take on the role of ministering to those under our
direct leadership.

Supporting Activities

In addition to what we have already discussed, there are supporting
activities involved in being a servant-leader. One is to prepare people
for expanded ministry—as God would define it for them.

We should meet with each person we are leading and jointly create a development plan aimed at God's unique vision for that
person. After creating the plan, coaching and training are natural
next steps to making sure the plan happens. Periodically evaluating
progress, which is part of coaching, will keep the plan in the person's
mind. Encouraging each person we lead will help him or her stay
energized and focused.

Quality Results

A balanced view of accomplishing the purpose, mission, and unique
vision of the church while developing the servants will change what

leaders evaluate. When leaders focus on ministry and projects with people as a resource, then numbers, dollars, and trends become the basis for evaluation. The growth of those being led is then often pushed aside. When leaders focus on people, then the growth of the follower becomes the basis for evaluation. In such cases, the ministry process is often pushed aside. When leaders focus on both the growth of the people and the ministry process, then a new set of standards becomes the basis of evaluation—standards that include both people and process. Discovering the new set of standards would be a great exercise for the senior leadership of your church. We are confident it will include a balance of both the Great Commandments to love God and others, and the Great Commission to go and make disciples.

THE ENVIRONMENT

Usually when leaders think about environment, they consider items such as friendliness, safety, cleanliness, colors, light, and comfortableness. As important as those things are, we will focus on a value environment.

Many churches we visit emphasize finding volunteers to do the ministry. Some churches announce the need for volunteers from the front during a worship service. Some churches have campaigns to fill the various ministry slots needed to keep the church running smoothly. The large majority of the time, communication centers on finding people to step up and help. Some use excitement, guilt, warning, and pressure.

Churches with servant-leaders focus on the person while leading the ministry process. In churches with servant-leaders, there is a constant awareness of the people: where they are in their walk with God, their knowledge of his Word, their skills and experiences, and their hopes and fears. That information is then used and balanced with the needs of the church as a body. It is not only about getting ministry done. It is also about developing people. This is the type of environment that true servant-leaders try to foster in the churches they lead.

PROVIDING FOR GROWTH

Outside of spiritual problems in the church and negative economic conditions in the community, there are two primary reasons that can cause a church to reach and stay on a plateau or start to decline. Those two reasons are a facility that can hold no more people and an over-worked leadership. If the facility has no more room, there are several potential solutions: hold more services each week, move to or build a larger facility, create a new church with some of the members, thereby reducing the number of people attending, or create a number of house churches in strategic locations around your community.

More critical is overworked leadership. Tired and hurting, Moses found his load far too much for him to handle. His father-in-law, Jethro, approached him with some great advice; Moses needed more leadership help. Even in the days of Moses, overworked leadership was an issue.

To provide for and to maintain growth over a long period, con-gregations must have adequate leadership in place, which will require a leadership-development program to prepare new leader-ship talent to replace those who leave or die, as well as to fill newly created jobs as the need arises. A quality leadership-development ministry does not happen accidentally; leadership needs to make it happen intentionally.

One of the easily ignored steps in leadership development is prac-tice. For people to develop their leadership skills, they need to lead. However, for the church it is a win-win situation. We are able to give them leadership-development responsibilities that fit their skill levels and at the same time have their growing skill as a reserve to grow the church.

LOVING PEOPLE, NOT USING PEOPLE

In the last chapter, we concluded that a leader's walk with Christ is central to his or her love for God and for people, as well as knowing God's will.

In this chapter, we concluded from Scripture that leaders have two roles: (1) to be a steward or agent for Christ, leading as Christ's representative, and (2) to be a servant, serving those being led, keeping the two roles in balance.

In the next chapter, we will be wrestling with the times when it seems that God is saying *no*.

CHAPTER 7

WHEN GOD SAYS NO

Finding God's specific plan for one's life challenges every Christian. Christian leaders often thrive under the challenge of "hearing the voice of the Lord in specific matters." Determining the will of God and his guidance for a group of people carries huge responsibilities. How is it that one can hear the voice of God and say to others, "The Lord spoke to me, this is the plan"? Let us look at an experience in the life of Paul and Silas that opens new horizons in understanding God's ways of guiding his people. As we look, an interesting question awaits us. What happens when God says no?

Paul the apostle had been leading missionary work for half a dozen years. Since being commissioned by the Holy Spirit during his stay in Antioch (Acts 13:1–3), his life had been a whirlwind. Now well into his second missionary journey in northwestern Asia, a puzzling experience confronted Paul. The same Holy Spirit who had commissioned him and his team to leave Antioch for regions unknown resisted his plan of operation. Acts 16 records that the Spirit of Jesus and the Holy Spirit "would not let them" go farther into Asia.

> Paul and his companions traveled throughout the region
> of Phrygia and Galatia, having been kept by the Holy

> Spirit from preaching the word in the province of Asia. When they came to the border of Mysia, they tried to enter Bithynia, but the Spirit of Jesus would not allow them to. So they passed by Mysia and went down to Troas. During the night Paul had a vision of a man of Macedonia standing and begging him, "Come over to Macedonia and help us." After Paul had seen the vision, we got ready at once to leave for Macedonia, concluding that God had called us to preach the gospel to them. (Acts 16:6–10)

The text does not say how God said no. However, it is clear that Paul had attempted to go in a specific, preplanned direction, and his efforts and leadership were stopped. First, Paul was listening and responding to the Holy Spirit. He was sensitive to God's voice and leadership. Second, God did delay and even prevent Paul from certain activities.

Just as God kept the lions' mouths shut and preserved Daniel's life, he sometimes keeps us silent until an opportune time. Just recently, we heard the story of an Indian immigrant who was working as an engineer in London. For some years, his Christian coworker had not said anything to him about Jesus Christ or spiritual matters. Then at a certain point, his coworker began asking him spiritual questions and inviting him to church. It was this timing that was strategic in what the Holy Spirit was doing in his life. And those conversations at a specific time were used by God to bring him to salvation. God opens and closes opportunities for the gospel. God does prevent and delay certain experiences in our lives because he is all-knowing and all-wise.

In 1992, Kevin Palau asked me (Tim) to visit the island nation of Jamaica. The pastors from the evangelical alliance had sent a letter of invitation to Luis Palau to conduct a national evangelistic festival. Kevin informed me that an invitation had come some seven years before, but it was determined that the timing was not of the Lord. Since the Luis Palau Association had specific biblical criteria for accepting invitations for ministry, their ability to say no was a wise choice. We need to remember that not all opportunities are God's voice telling us to move in a certain direction.

The Ugly Word No

As God speaks to his people, they need to realize that no is in his vocabulary. We can embrace that no with a positive attitude. For the moment, no may seem disheartening. But in the long run, no can bring many positive results. Many times the Bible tells us what we should not do or how we should not act. The purpose of God's instruction has the goal to protect, to instruct, and to build up; not to tear down. When the Bible tells fathers "do not exasperate your children" (Eph. 6:4), it is a corrective statement. The purposes include stopping abuse, promoting a positive spirit within the children, building a better relationship between father and children, and helping the children to understand God as a father who helps them.

If we are to hear the voice of God, then we need to embrace the noes that come our way. The Ten Commandments are a classic example of the voice of God directing all people into healthy relationships. The "thou shalt nots" of these commands are to show us that tragic consequences follow disobedient behaviors. Certainly, the linguistic style of these commands is not the point. Rather, the fact that God says, "Do not do this," speaks volumes to the selfish and rebellious hearts of the fallen race. We, in our flesh, just don't like anyone telling us no. Yet God corrects our attitudes and behaviors while confronting us in a direct way.

When No Is a Good Thing

We want to put a positive slant on the fact that God says no to us. God does love us enough to direct us with a no. And he can do so through a variety of ways: through his direct statements in the Bible, through our conscience that he created, through the decision of the people of God as they wait on him, or through the voice of God to us on an amoral issue. The experience of Paul in Acts 16 and the stories of our own journeys reveal that no has positive and productive outcomes.

Paul and his companions took the no as an opportunity to stop and listen. As they waited on the Lord, a new vision came; in this case, a vision in the night. Whether by dream or trance, the text does not say. But Paul woke the next day with a clear and compelling reason for changing his ministry direction and strategy. This vision in Paul's journey is often referred to as "the Macedonian call."

The power of this vision still touches our hearts today. Here is a man who is begging. Picture a strong man pleading for all he is worth for Paul to hear and respond to his pleading. On the one hand, there is not a more pitiful sight than a man begging, pleading, and crying out, "Come help us!" Men are supposed to be strong, self-sufficient, proud, capable, independent, but now here is a humble man, pleading for himself and a whole continent of people that have no hope. He is their ambassador, seeking to gain what no one else can get.

Can't you picture this? A young yet physically buff man with the veins of his neck bulging as he cups his hands in front of his mouth and yells at the top of his voice, "Hey, Paul, look over here!" He then waves his strong arm motioning Paul to come his way. Then he speaks with a pleading voice, "See the children, see the women, see the young and old, rich and poor; we are without Christ, without hope. Please come and tell us the good news! Please, we have never heard! Come quickly, many are dying without Christ! Come now, come today, and, oh, please come!"

We have observed that when a believer hears God saying no, he often takes it the wrong way. We're not referring to no in the case of the moral issues of life, but no in the area of guidance and ministry. These are noes from the Holy Spirit regarding ministry opportunities, vocational choices, places to live or work, what to buy or own, timing issues, etc. Some take no as God saying, "I do not believe in you." Or some might believe that God says no because of some sin in the past. God has set this person aside and can no longer use him for kingdom work.

For example, I (Tim) clearly remember my friendship with a man who was a committed follower of Jesus. He was twenty years my senior and displayed a real passion for God. He had married in his early twenties, but the marriage did not work and ended in divorce. Since that experience, he had felt that God and the church had placed a sign reading "second-class citizen" over his head. Though for many years he was faithful to the church, had married again to a lovely Christian woman, and lived a committed life to Jesus, he seemed blocked from taking on new roles of ministry. I have often thought of the many Christians living with this "second-class" mentality, not yet able to embrace the grace and forgiveness of God. Yet, so often, the church has not extended the same forgiveness God has. Often we have incorrectly interpreted God's no to the detriment of other people. God forgives sin completely. And he does not say no as a reminder of our failures in the past.

WHEN NO MEANS YES

What the story of Paul in Acts 16 teaches is that no means yes, but not here (this direction), not now (timing), and not in this way (methodology). God directs his people to where they should be serving him. It does matter to God where we serve or do not serve him. Though Lot thought Sodom and Gomorrah were good places to live, the Lord did not think so. Places do matter.

Jesus ministered in Galilee for a time. In this context, he trained others to follow him and serve his kingdom. On at least two occasions, he informed those who went out to preach the gospel of the kingdom to minister where they were welcomed and cared for. That is, minister in those places where people are responsive (Luke 9:1–9; 10:1–16).

In our own journeys, we have on a number of occasions sought to serve the Lord in one particular setting, yet the journeys "did not work out" because the Lord had another place of service for us. "Not here" may mean geography, or it may be addressing the people being ministered to, or a particular role in ministry. We need to be open to God's leading as to the place of ministry.

LEARNING THE TIMING OF GOD

Another issue addressed in serving the Lord is the issue of timing. Paul had been reaching those in Asia who had not heard the gospel when he realized God had another place for him to go. Paul did not seem particularly sensitive to the timing of God. It does not appear he was thinking that it was now time to leave this place and go to another place. He does not seem to be suffering from the "grass is greener" syndrome. He and his team were busy about making the gospel known in Asia. So the Lord Jesus had to "get their attention."

We would love to know how the Spirit of Jesus and the Holy Spirit arrested their attention. How was it that the Holy Spirit "kept" them and then later "would not allow them" (Acts 16:6–7) to preach the gospel in the province of Asia and Mysia? Was there no interest on the part of the population there? Did Paul and his team get physically sick? Was there some type of natural disaster (earthquake, windstorm, etc.)? All we know is that Paul had to stop and wait (timing issue) upon the Lord.

One of the great stresses in family life is what sociologists call natural or normal family life-cycle events. The normal time for marriage is between twenty and thirty years of age. Marriage before or after creates certain stresses upon the family system if the "timing" is not on schedule. Abraham and Sarah were too old to have children (biologically their clocks had run out of time). The unfolding of the drama of Genesis related to this issue is well known. God showed his power and sovereignty in their lives. Abraham and Sarah showed their fleshliness and lack of trust in God, as no doubt any of us would do or have done. Timing relates to trusting God. God said to Paul in Acts 16, "Not now."

One could say NOW is the time, but not here. We can be people who either have our heads in the sand or are looking for greener pastures and often, in either case, miss the leading of God in our lives. We are dealing particularly with God leading his church. When are we to change, or hold the course, or add a new ministry, or stop a certain ministry, or add staff? *When* is a word that addresses the issue of timing. Therefore, we must walk in a listening relationship with God and those whom we serve in order to discern the *now* of God.

MINISTRY METHODS DO CHANGE

A third question focuses on adopting new methodologies. New methodologies address the way or manner in which something is done. Paul had been working with a certain team and preaching the gospel initially to the Jews in Gentile cities. Now, following the departure of Barnabas and John Mark (Acts 15:39–40), Paul was developing a new team (Timothy, Silas, and Luke). This new team was now composed of Gentiles (Luke and Timothy), creating a multiethnic group. With this new team, there came a new place of ministry (Europe) and a new methodology. A change from the synagogue to the place of prayer, as the context of ministering the gospel, came with their transition from Asia to Europe. Not a huge change—still seeking the spiritually sensitive—but nonetheless a different place, a new place for ministry.

The methodologies expanded greatly when Paul arrived in Athens. There he added dialogue and debate to his normal preaching and teaching in the synagogues and places of prayer. In fact, these new methods made the ministry more effective in the new culture of Europe. Paul "reasoned in the synagogue with the Jews and the God-fearing Greeks, as well as in the *marketplace* day by day with those who happened to be there" (Acts 17:17).

HOW DOES GOD GUIDE THE CHURCH?

God guides his people by confronting their comfort zones and complacencies with a startling two-letter word: *no*. However, the church can go for years and decades without hearing God's no. We tend to justify old methodologies and forms. We seem to hang on to the "old wineskins" as if they are the power of God rather than a form through which God expresses himself for a moment in time. The noes of God need to gain our attention. How can one identify them? Again, this is not a moral area. This question deals with the effectiveness and relevance of the gospel in any culture at any particular time.

One way of understanding when God says yes or no comes simply in measuring a particular ministry or method's effectiveness. Is anyone coming? Are people interested? Are we addressing real needs? Are we answering a question that is being asked? Are we thinking relationally? Are we missing something? What is being overlooked?

One of the first Luis Palau crusades I (Tim) attended was in Des Moines, Iowa, in October of 1990. The crusade was held in the heart of the city at the downtown convention center. I was new on the team and anxious to learn all I could. I not only conversed with a number of staff and local committee members directly, but also did my share of eavesdropping to hear what people were "really saying." On several occasions, the executive committee members shared what they were seeing God do not only in the crusade, but also before and during the crusade in relationship-building among the leaders of the city. Additionally, the story of how God was bringing these leaders together in new ministry alliances often came to my ears. While the evangelical churches had moved to the suburbs over the past ten to fifteen years, the heart of that city had become neglected. However, in the process of working together on the crusade, being held in the heart of the city, leaders once again saw the great needs in the heart of their city. God was saying to them, "You have forgotten the center of your city." So in a subtle yet clear rebuke, a number of leaders renewed their commitments to the urban portions of their city. God guides by showing us what we are not doing. His voice of rebuke can correct our selfish ways and restore us to areas of great need and productive ministry.

NEW AND INNOVATIVE IDEAS

God guides the church not only through subtle or overt rebukes, but also through new and innovative ideas. One benefit the church derives from its younger members is the creative ideas they often bring to the ministry setting. The young have a reputation of being radical, random, and obnoxious. However, youth are often the conduit for the passion of the gospel, and they have a willingness to embrace "new wineskins." For this, we should all be thankful. Today the emerging church movement has embraced many new methodologies for packaging the gospel in ways that make sense to the youth in our culture. The "medium is the message" has far more power than we would like to ascribe to it. Yet Jesus said, "By this all men will know that you are my disciples, if you love one another" (John 13:35). This was no one-liner in a pop song, but a description of radical Christianity. A message from the Master that said our actions do speak louder than our words. With no action to back up our words, our words sound very hollow. Yet our unwillingness to embrace new methodologies often leads to the demise of our churches.

When our churches are committed to relevance, our message never changes, but our methods are adapted for effective communication of the gospel. Truth and love are our guiding principles, the methods are only a means of delivery. As Luis Palau has often said, "I do not necessarily like the music [of a Palau festival], but I love the kids who like the music."[1] In order to adopt new methods, we need freedom from the fears that lurk in the shadows of our unsanctified memories. In chapter 8, we will deal with fear as a roadblock to ministry growth and development. We must all remind ourselves that the message of the gospel never changes, but the understanding of the culture should always shape our methods.

Let's review. Not now, not here, and not in this way are three guiding principles behind the Lord telling us no. Here we are discussing ministry opportunities and strategies. God does say no from time to time. God actively guides us if we will only listen and will not be disheartened by the noes he sends our way. Rather we should stop and listen. We should ask ourselves, "If not here, where? If not now, when? If not in this way, how?"

Two helpful principles will guide us in answering these questions.

THE GREATEST NEED

First, where is the greatest need? Where are people crying out for help? Where is there an urgent appeal for the good news? Where is there an absence of the love of Christ? Where are the responsive? There are substantial biblical examples to indicate that a determining factor in selecting a ministry setting should include the responsiveness of the people.

Paul's experience demonstrates that the gospel needs to go where it has never gone before. Many ask, "Why should so many have multiple opportunities to hear and receive the gospel when many have not yet had one opportunity?" A dear friend, Dr. Bill Thomas, often says of his own focus of ministry selection, "I go to where the call is the loudest and the need is the greatest." Paul and his team were responding to the cry of a desperate man.

Therefore, when we ask ourselves about where God might be calling us to serve him, we need to include in our meditations the question "Where is the greatest need?" The answer to this question could involve geography, relationships, and/or personal interest, such as people who are new to our neighborhoods and cities. For example, in China today, twenty-five million people move from the country to the city each year. This presents an opportunity for ministry to many organizations that deal with humanitarian and social needs. Many American cities are also undergoing substantial demographic change. Therefore, we need to be asking, "Where are people most vulnerable to the changes in their lives? What people are open to new relationships? What specific needs can we address for these people? How has God uniquely equipped us to meet these needs?" (We have knowledge, skills, money, etc., that makes us a resource to others without these resources.)

New Team Members

Second, where is the team? Who wants to serve? Who is willing to go? Whom has God brought to work with us? The makeup of the team affects how ministry will be done. God's sovereign deployment of workers into the harvest often addresses how the ministry will be done. In Acts 16, Paul had a new team. One new member was Luke, a physician. Luke had a strategic role in applying the art of medicine. Both Paul and Silas were in need of medical attention not many days after their journey began. In Philippi, Paul and Silas were attacked by a crowd, dragged before the Roman officials, severely flogged, and thrown into prison (Acts 16:22–24). Though miraculously released, they were no doubt in need of Dr. Luke's assistance. God provides through the team skills, talents, and spiritual gifts that will equip the team for what is needed.

In determining the place, timing, and methodologies of ministry, we need to assess the team, for God works through his people. How has God outfitted our team? What are the unique gifts, talents, experiences, and passions of our church family? Ministry flows through relationships. When we wonder what God wants us to do, we need to evaluate the team God has brought.

In the mideighties, while I (Tim) was a pastor of a church in Southern California, I welcomed a new couple into our church. Not long after meeting them, I had the opportunity to lead the husband to join our ministry of visiting those in the hospital. Dick eagerly received my mentoring and faithfully visited those persons that I asked him to see. Dick quickly understood that the Lord was using him in a special way. He delighted in cheering people up. He enjoyed praying with them, and reports came my way of how much the people enjoyed Dick's cheerful visits. A significant ministry developed for Dick as his joy in ministry helped him recruit others. Identifying an interest, giving knowledge and skill in ministry, modeling ministry, and encouraging Dick brought a new level of service not only for Dick, but also for many others in the church.

God says no to us from time to time. This may be to rebuke us, but it also can be to direct us into new seasons of strategic ministry. So when your ministry runs into an unexpected resistance, stop and pray. Take some time to wait upon the Lord and see if there is some new place, new focus, or new way of serving him. Maybe no—or maybe yes, but not here, not now, or not in this way.

CHAPTER 8

A GOOD KIND OF FEAR

Fear can paralyze our emotions or mobilize us for great acts of faith. I (Tim) had such an experience during Christmas vacation almost a decade ago. My son was then seventeen. He was a dedicated athlete, lifted weights, played several sports, and was always in top physical form. However, he has battled with asthma since he was three years of age.

Our family had been visiting our California relatives over the Christmas holidays. The night before we were scheduled to start our journey home to Portland, Oregon, Joel had an asthma attack, and I rushed him to Mercy Hospital in Bakersfield. This was a very scary scene for me. Joel was desperately gasping for air. The doctors ordered a "cocktail" of medications. The emergency-room nurse gave him one dose, and then a second. The dosage was too much. It acted as an over-dose. I'd never seen reaction to medication like it. I stood over my son's bed as his chest was heaving and his heart racing, and I had a sense that his heart was going to burst. That was a fearful moment, a helpless moment, and a time when my emotions were paralyzed.

Fear has many faces. Fear comes in many forms. I remember taking a group of Christians to the Holy Land in 1984. We went to Israel, Egypt, Greece, and Turkey. We were in Cairo on a beautiful spring day. Our group was touring the pyramids. We had the opportunity to

111

climb right into the heart of the pyramid. The passage was extremely narrow with one person on the heels of the next, plodding one tediously slow step after another up a rickety wooden ladder.

My dad shuffled up the ladder just a few people in front of me. He was doing well for a man in his midsixties. Suddenly he said, "I've got to get out of here." We stopped as he reversed his direction and scurried down. He was overcome with claustrophobia. His claustrophobia stemmed from his working career as a plumber in Shafter, California, where the soil is extremely sandy. He had experienced a number of cave-ins in which he had been buried alive. He'd gotten out on each occasion, but that pyramid was too close to "being like a ditch." So he had to find the quickest way of escape.

What Are Your Fears?

We each deal with some (or many!) fears. Fear of failure, rejection, death, change, lack of money, responsibility, people, the future, success—the list is quite unlimited. Fears come to us in various forms throughout life. Psalm 34 chronicles the emotional journey of a soul tormented with fears of all kinds. David's paranoia manifests itself in his making bad decisions, uncontrolled hysteria, and total dominance by his emotions over his mental capacities. David exhibited abruptness with God and behavior that was totally out of control.

Chapters 20 and 21 of 1 Samuel reveal the context of this painful story. David and Jonathan had developed a sign language signaling whether Saul intended to kill David or not. Just imagine the drama of that late-afternoon rendezvous. David's young life hung in the balance. So much was at stake. David's life flashed in front of him. What would happen?

David contemplated his relationship with Jonathan, his best friend. They had gone through so much in just a few short years. Jonathan had defended him, repeatedly spoken up for him, and attempted to convince Saul that David was a loyal servant. David and Jonathan's hearts beat as one. They found great motivation in their friendship. No other relationship had comparable like-mindedness. They truly had a wonderful relationship that meant the world to both of them. However, because of Saul's paranoia, power, and evil intentions, their relationship had to be severed.

So in 1 Samuel 21, we see David running. He runs to the priest at Nob. When he gets to the place of worship, he addresses Ahimelech the priest: "Do you have any bread?" "Well no, I don't have any regular bread. We just have the special bread, the bread for worship, and you can't have that." David argues with and then pressures the priest until he gets the bread. Then he says, "Do you have a sword, a spear, any weapon?" Ahimelech responds, "Actually, I have Goliath's sword—the one you used to kill him." So in his state of panic, enhanced by his recent loss of relationship with Jonathan, the only thing that he can think about is food and a weapon. The story omits anything about God or prayer. He grabs the two things he believes will save his life, food and a weapon, as he runs off to Gath.

From Bad to Worse

David's situation was like jumping out of the frying pan into the fire. It seems he was thinking to himself, *Well, they know that I'm an enemy of Saul. And Saul's the king of Israel. So if I run and join them, they'll think that I'm on their side, and they'll rescue me and they will take care of me.* But to his great surprise, when he got to Gath, the people said, "Isn't this David, the king of the land? Isn't he the one they sing about in their dances: 'Saul has slain his thousands, and David his tens of thousands'?" (1 Sam. 21:11). David's paranoia had blinded him to the realities of the day. He was well known, and he was not going to find safety from the enemies of Israel. He hoped for safety and rest. He found that he had run into the hands of the enemy.

See what fear does? See what happens when we are not focused on the Lord and the joy of the Lord even in the midst of great danger?

Every day there are people, events, and circumstances that can overwhelm us. Fear raises its ugly head to frighten us and block us from
trusting the Lord.

In the early 1990s, I (Tim) visited Taiwan for the first time in preparation for a Luis Palau crusade. Traveling alone to a new country,
staying in unfamiliar missionary housing in Taipei, one of the most
densely populated cities in the world, I found little comfort in this
overbearing city. Not knowing a soul in the city, I became even lone-
lier as I reflected on what my host said as he dropped me off: "I'll pick
you up in a day or so." I did not speak Chinese. I had little money. But
there I was, surrounded by the unfamiliar and all alone.

At least I was inside, out of the smog and fog of Taipei. But it was
a terrible night. I've never been more paranoid or sensed such darkness. Actually, I am a little scared of the dark. I was anxious, irritated,
and could not sleep. I called back home to talk to my wife two or three
times during the night. Somehow, I got through a night that seemed
like an eternity.

At the end of my trip, Doug Cannon, a missionary friend that I
have known for a number of years, picked me up and took me to the
airport. As I described this experience to him, I said, "I've never had
such terrifying feelings like this. Why this fear, this overwhelming
sense of darkness and paranoia?"

Listening thoughtfully, he replied, "You know this country has
given itself to worshipping spirits of their deceased family members.
There is substantial demon worship and activity throughout this
land." Some of our fears originate because of spiritual warfare, some
fears from broken relationships, and some from our own personal
abuses.

The historical context of Psalm 34 suggests that David was overcome with fear. Fear can apply amazing amounts of negative pressure
upon our souls, and like David, we can make very unwise decisions.

Leaders and managers of the affairs of our Lord will need to address
these subtle or overt fears if we are to be fruitful in ministry. When our
inner motivations come from fear and not faith, we will ultimately

prove powerless in seeing the kingdom of Jesus transform our world. If we do not face the reality of the fears within, then we will masquerade as sufficient saints when in fact we are quite inadequate for life and leadership. Some may hide behind an attitude of superiority, using titles and degrees to impress others. Others will avoid issues of personal need and growth by blaming others, changing the subject, or delegating to staff issues that they should handle themselves. This pseudo-Christianity typically crumbles under the pressures and strains of life.

The Way of Escape

How did David get out of this mess? He pretended he was insane. He acted like a madman. He drooled on his beard, looked crazy, and acted weird. His great theatrical performance convinced the king to let him go. When the king saw David, he said, "This is a crazy man. I have enough crazy Gathites. I don't need one more. Get him out of here." So David fled again, this time in a safer direction. Fear leads to fleeing. Running from life's problems indicates fear is the motivation, not faith. Lack of trust in the Lord and calling out to him for wisdom and deliverance cost David many moments of peace.

Maybe we are running from something. Only we—and God—know what is bothering us, regardless of the anxieties we have. But Psalm 34 comes to comfort the stressed out, the anxious, the tired, the burned out. Christian leaders must learn early in ministry that, until we can confront and control personal fear, we will not stand in the face of testing.

Five Realities of Dealing with Fear

1. There Are Fears

Psalm 34:4 says, "I sought the LORD, and he answered me; he delivered me from all my fears." Verse 6 says, "This poor man called, and the

LORD heard him; he saved him out of all his troubles." Verses 17–19 declare, "He delivers them from all their troubles. The LORD is close to the brokenhearted and saves those who are crushed in spirit. A righteous man may have many troubles, but the LORD delivers him from them all."

Here the Hebrew text graphically describes the distraught condition of David. His fears span a kaleidoscope of emotions. His soul was sorely troubled. He was overanxious. The sense of the word in verse 6, "troubles," portrays a picture of terror. He was horrified. He was shaking in his boots. The saliva had dribbled out all over his beard. Terror had gripped David's soul. These graphic words paint an ugly picture of those emotions that paralyzed his faith.

2. Fears Can Overcome Us

Think of Peter, walking on the water in the midst of the Sea of Galilee, focusing on Jesus. All of a sudden, Peter took his eyes off Jesus and looked at the winds and the waves. What happened? He began to sink until Jesus lifted him up. Or think of Elisha's servant in 2 Kings 6, who woke up one morning and looked out and saw 180,000 Assyrians surrounding him. He was petrified. He could not see until Elisha said, "Lord, open his eyes." Any number of fears could be in front of us. It could be fear for our children, marriage, ministry, lack of significance, a hidden sin, or fear that there won't be enough money to get through the month. When we focus on our fears and anxieties, they can overwhelm us. Thinking only about the problems, the anxieties, and the what-ifs can so paralyze our thinking that we become immobile.

Just a few years ago, some dear friends were completely at wits' end over their adopted teenage daughter. She was a very intelligent and gifted young woman. However, her self-imposed standards of performance had driven her to an anorexic condition. She began to lose an unhealthy number of pounds. She had heart failure at one point because of her extreme weight loss. The parents did all they knew how to do. But the behaviors worsened. In their community of faith, they continued to share and be open to the support of other Christian friends. At one point, they were so immobilized they literally could not make a decision. The fear of losing their daughter overwhelmed them. As the community acted for them, the Lord brought amazing healing and health to their daughter. Fear can paralyze faith.

The good news, however, comes when one overcomes these fears by embracing "the fear of the Lord." Psalm 34:9 says, "Fear the LORD, you his saints, for those who fear him lack nothing." What is this? Human fears, fears that come to us, fears that melt our hearts, fears that get us focused on things other than what God has called us to, and fears that keep his joy from residing in our hearts are overcome by another kind of fear. An awe of God, a reverence for God, a deep confidence in him—that is what gives us hope. Our God is bigger than all our human fears.

3. We Need to Embrace the Fear of the Lord

The fear of the Lord is an action of praising our amazing God. The fear of the Lord places us in a dynamic tension that, on one hand, causes us to tremble, yet at the same time, draws us closer to him because of his goodness and his grace.

One of C. S. Lewis's characters in the Chronicles of Narnia portrays this dynamic tension. Peter and Lucy, two of the main characters, were going to be introduced to Aslan, the lion. They had just finished a long and tiresome journey. Eventually they came to an extensive valley filled with creatures of all shapes and sizes. As they walked into this lush valley, they got their first glimpse of this glorious, gigantic, breathtaking lion. This tension becomes a dynamic feeling in the pit of Peter's stomach that causes him to shake. But then the lion speaks in his huge, melodious voice, drawing Peter right into his presence. Peter, though fearful, is captured by the love he sees in the eyes of the lion and hears in his compassionate voice. Fear is replaced by faith. What would have caused Peter and Lucy to run and hide melted in the face of this irresistible goodness.

Psalm 34:9 commands, "Fear the LORD, you his saints, for those who fear him lack nothing." David had gotten his focus totally off the

Lord. He had panicked. He was fleeing. He was running. He was doing ridiculous things. When our anxieties overwhelm us, we make bad decisions. When our faith is not focused on the Lord, we can do really stupid things—even as believers in Jesus Christ.

The fear of the Lord must be learned, as described in verse 11, "Come, my children, listen to me; I will teach you the fear of the LORD." You need to *learn* how to fear the Lord. To fear the Lord is not automatic. It does not just come to us naturally. David, speaking out of his own experience with fear and paranoia, is saying, "Let me teach you about the fear of the Lord."

How then does one learn to fear the Lord? Look at verses 1–3. "I will extol the LORD at all times; his praise will always be on my lips. My soul will boast in the LORD; let the afflicted hear and rejoice. Glorify the LORD with me; let us exalt his name together." *We fear the Lord when we praise him.* We overcome anxieties, worries, and paranoia when we praise the Lord. That is why our souls are desperate for corporate worship. We cannot live without being with his people and in his presence. There is nothing like it. To praise the Lord means to boast about him, to brag about him, to elevate and shout aloud praises to his name. To praise the Lord means you will forget about yourself. Worship requires that we bring all our mental and emotional capacities to focus upon the living and true God. We are cheerleaders for him, because he is worthy of all praise.

Verse 4 states, "I sought the LORD, and he answered me; he delivered me from all my fears." Verse 6 adds, "This poor man called, and the LORD heard him." Verse 17 says, "The righteous cry out, and the LORD hears them." *We fear the Lord by seeking him diligently through prayer.* By pursuing God, our minds focus on the greatest goal of all. By determining that we *will* find him and no other demonstrates our devotion to him. We forsake all others, focusing upon him only. By seeking him in prayer, we gain a new perspective. When we pray, the Lord becomes the source and resource for our lives. Prayer demonstrates respect and dependency. He is the one we trust and rely upon. Prayer communicates our delight in the

Lord. Prayer is personal, conversational, and intimate. God delights in hearing from his children.

Verses 13 and 14 say in part, "keep your tongue from evil ... seek peace and pursue it." What is the fear of the Lord? *It is a righteous life. Not a self-righteous, but an upright and holy life.* A life lived in dependence upon him. A life that chooses to be true, honest, loyal, kind, and loving conquers fear. How do we fear the Lord? How does the Lord know that we fear him? When we live like his Son and make the choices his Son would make.

Finally, *to fear the Lord we need to view the eternal as more important than the temporary.* Isaiah said centuries ago, "The righteous pass away; the godly often die before their time. And no one seems to care or wonder why. No one seems to understand that God is protecting them from the evil to come. For the godly who die will rest in peace" (Isa. 57:1–2 NLT). Those who fear the Lord have a proper biblical expectation that the righteous are with the Lord and in his presence.

So what have we learned so far? That we can fear the Lord by praising him with our lips, by seeking him in diligent prayer, by living a holy life, and by maintaining a heavenly perspective. The next part of this psalm gives us a cause to smile.

4. The Fear of the Lord Produces a Radiant Countenance

What does the fear of the Lord produce in the life of one who believes, the one who has faith in God? What was the outcome of David's experience, after all of his fear, running, and insanity? Verse 5 says, "Those who look to him are radiant; their faces are never covered with shame." What does the fear of the Lord produce in the life of a believer? *A radiant countenance reveals a heart that trusts the Lord,* reflecting his presence in the midst of it all.

When I (Tim) was in the third grade, the Lord brought a wonderful Christian woman into my life to be my Sunday-school teacher, first as my "Jet Cadet" leader in elementary school, then again as my junior high advisor. I will never forget her. As a youthful adult even in her midforties, she loved adventure. She led many youth outings to the beach and mountains. On many occasions, there was Mary with a carload of teenagers. Mary became a living saint to me. When I think of the radiance of Jesus, I see Mary's face. She always had a big smile and a happy spirit.

But it wasn't just a natural smile to me—she had a special glow. She was the first person to teach me about the Spirit-filled life. I remember her talks on Romans chapters 6 and 7. She used a state-of-the-art visual aid—flannelgraph. Her teaching began to click with me concerning my need to yield my life to Christ on a daily basis, walking in the power of his Spirit.

Although she had ample physical and financial resources, Mary's life was very difficult. I learned later in life that she had a very trying marriage. But despite her troubles, I never saw her without a smile.

Those who fear the Lord have a radiant countenance. Verse 8 says, "Taste and see that the LORD is good; blessed is the man who takes refuge in him." Experiencing the goodness of the Lord brings an inner joy that breaks forth on our faces. Knowing and being known by the Lord is his great desire. God invites us to taste and see that he is good. What's the result of those who fear the Lord? They know that God is good. They experience him. He experiences them. They delight in one another.

5. The Fear of the Lord Produces Freedom

Psalm 34:22 says, "The LORD redeems his servants; no one will be condemned who takes refuge in him." What does the fear of the Lord produce in the life of a believer? *A life uncondemned, experiencing freedom, joy, and hope.* "Therefore, there is now no condemnation for those who are in Christ Jesus, because through Christ Jesus the law of the Spirit of life set me free from the law of sin and death" (Rom. 8:1–2). Those who fear the Lord are those who live an uncondemned life. We pray that, as leaders, we will guard our hearts from the fears of the Evil One and every day we will choose to fear the Lord.

Jan was a high school classmate of mine (Tim). She was the vale-dictorian of our class. She went on to a Christian university. In her professional life, Jan became a ghostwriter for many very prominent authors. She attained very high positions and received a PhD in liter-ature from a major university. At one point in her life, she married a Christian young man. When they returned from their honeymoon, he informed her, "I don't want to be married to you."

As a young woman in her twenties, Jan had a choice. She could have given in to a broken heart and turned on life as a cruel joke. But instead she accepted the tragedy of the moment as from the Lord, and trusting in him, she has lived a happy and productive life. She said to me as we shared a dinner together, "I made a choice that I wouldn't allow that sorrow to fill my heart, but rather, I would serve the Lord." And the Lord has honored her with a tremendous and effective ministry.

Life has many choices. For leaders in the church of Jesus Christ, the fears within can paralyze us and keep us from accomplishing fruitful ministry. Some top executives in America were asked, "What has motivated you to such great accomplishments in your business?" The majority answered, "I fear failure." What a way to live life—dominated by fear of failure. But how different for those of us who follow Jesus Christ! Not fear of failure, but great respect and awe of God drives us! The fear of the Lord is the beginning of wisdom, and a life lived with his love drives out every unwanted fear.

This is what the church needs—leaders free from fear and filled with the love of God.

CHAPTER 9

HELPING OTHERS DEAL WITH FEAR

One day while watching a mother and her young son at the swimming pool, a few of us relished his grand time sitting by the edge of the water and splashing everyone around him. The boy went over to the steps and, after walking down a couple of steps, stood in the pool up to his waist.

Oh, how brave he believed himself to be.

Caught up in her son's newfound bravery, the mother scooped up her son and planted him on the side of the pool, encouraging him to jump into her arms. She promised she would catch him. He crouched down as if he were about to jump.

Then as if he had suddenly come to his senses, he paused. He stood there wanting to be brave and jump. Repeatedly, he would get ready to leap and each time his mother would brace to catch him, only to have him back away.

That particular day, his mother could not get him to jump. They left the pool with the mother upset because her son would not jump and the boy upset because his mother was angry with him.

The time at the pool for the mother and son should have been a great adventure. Because of the son's fear and the mother's inability to help her son through the fear, the day was a disaster for both.

INSIDIOUS FEAR

Fear is an insidious, subtle, limiting, and seldom understood emotion. Paralyzing fear like this small boy felt can be just as disabling to adults. The problem does not stop with the one experiencing the fear. Inability to understand, let alone deal with, the fear of others can be just as frustrating for leaders as it was for that mother.

During the bank mergers that occurred in the early 1990s, many people received displacement notices. For them, the fear they experienced was understandable. The surprise was, however, that many of those who stayed with the merged company displayed the same fear as the employees displaced by the merger.

What caused them to be afraid?

How can leadership be part of the solution?

The answers to those questions rest in three principles:

1. People tend to freeze when it comes to leaving the familiar, even if the familiar is bad.
2. It is scary to face the unknown, even if you know it is better than what you have.
3. Change takes time, and the longer it takes, the harder it is to cope.

People Tend to Freeze When It Comes to Leaving the Familiar, Even if the Familiar Is Bad

You all know Carmen. Yes you do! She is the teller at your bank—been there for years. She always smiles at you and calls you by name when you come into the bank to make your deposit. Carmen is around forty, with short brown hair with just a little gray starting to show. She knows the names of all your kids and where you like to go for dinner. You saw her the other day at the supermarket and she remembered you. Carmen is a great woman, who just received bad news.

Just that morning, Carmen's boss told her that the bank was going to replace some of the tellers with automatic teller machines and she was going to be let go.

It is not as if she has not dreamed of getting out of there someday. Her boss is a pain in the neck, always yelling at her and everyone else for that matter. They cut her hours awhile back and took away her free parking and her health insurance. Now she has to take the bus and it takes an hour and a half to get there and the same to get home.

But Carmen is also a scared woman. She knows in her heart that she hates her job and really does not like her mean, abusive boss, but she has had that teller spot now for years. She eats upstairs, talking about kids and grandkids with people she knows well and who know her equally well. For years, she has had you for a customer, along with many others that she is comfortable with. She cares about you as a friend would.

It may not be the best situation, but it is what she does. It is where she works. It is almost who she is. The whole thought of leaving and no longer living the life she knows makes her freeze. It feels a little like death, and that is scary.

This same fear plagues the church whenever leadership decides it is time to take a new direction, such as changing the worship style. This is standard form for most rapidly dying churches. Both the leaders and the members may realize that whatever they are doing is chasing people away and they need to change, but it is still extremely difficult to make the change.

In chapter 1, Central Evangelical had to face that fear. In their case, they had the dilemma of facing the fear of the rebirth of the church and all its unknowns, or the fear of the church's death and the need for each of them to find a new church home.

It Is Scary to Face the Unknown, Even if We Know It Is Better Than What We Have

Bradon graduated from seminary a little more than a year ago. Unfortunately, jobs in youth ministry are hard to come by these days, so he has been working as a janitor in a local church to support his wife, Suzanne, and their little girl. Suzanne works part-time as a pediatric nurse at a local hospital. She really wants to stop working and have another baby but cannot because they need the money. Bradon does not mind the job. He mostly works alone and just does his job. It is actually a comfortable life, at least as far as responsibility is concerned. However, it is not the work for which he was trained.

When Bradon was in high school he was a natural leader, the one voted "most likely to succeed." He was always reluctant to take on a new challenge, but when he did, he was successful.

Now he is facing a job opportunity as a youth pastor in the church where he attends. This is not an ordinary youth pastor opportunity. That church has experienced four youth pastors in the last six years. This church chews up youth pastors and spits them out as a normal course. There are giants in that church that make Goliath look wimpy. This is what Bradon prepared for. Yet he is terrified.

What if he gets chewed up also? How does he handle these people? It pays more money than his janitor job, but what if he ends up losing the job like the previous youth pastors? What will he do then? Four pastors before him did not make it. It seems like certain failure.

There is little hope, and Bradon feels defeated before he even accepts the position. He just wants to curl up with his broom at the church and let the whole thing pass him by. Bradon is trapped between his fear of the unknown future and his desire to be an adequate husband, father, and soldier for Christ. He is frozen with indecision.

Fear of the unknown has kept many from following a call that God gave them or taking a role in the church when in their hearts they wanted to. Fear of the unknown silences believers from sharing their faith with their neighbors or giving their testimonies when asked.

Fear of the unknown cripples many evangelism thrusts. Churches will hold evangelism training to prepare people to share their faith, and little happens afterward.

Fear of the unknown kept that little boy from leaping into his mother's arms. Long before major change occurs in most organizations, leadership starts processing the change. They form committees and have meetings for months. They have time to begin looking for ways to protect themselves socially and emotionally long before the change becomes imminent.

Yet fear of the unknown is part of the problem within leadership that keeps them from stepping out to help others deal with their fears. The unknown that leaders are afraid of has less to do with the change they are preparing to meet and more to do with the fear of dealing with people who are scared. It is a ministry that few leaders are experienced in, and therefore, they will find many excuses not to follow through. More likely, they will simply ignore the need.

What happens when leadership announces a change to the staff? How do leaders and the nonleaders (staff and congregation) view each other? There is probably some level of distrust of the leaders. After all, the leaders appear comfortable and everyone else is uncomfortable.

The leaders become frustrated just as the mother was with her son. Can the staff and congregation not see the benefit? The leaders fail to understand the fear that everyone else is feeling, even though many of them felt the same fear months earlier. The leaders perceive the staff as acting like babies or rebellious brats. They told the staff and congregation that the change would become something good, just like the mother explained to her son that jumping would be fun. Just like the boy, the people of the church cannot ignore their fear. They have not yet had the opportunity to adjust to the idea.

What might this fear look like in the church setting? Let us address a circumstance found in many struggling churches.

For many years, Your Church has been slowly losing members. The leaders have decided that if they do not reverse the trend, the church will have to close its doors soon. Up to now, the condition has been obvious, but no one talks about it. The fear of facing the future keeps the problem hidden from discussion. The people avoid the fear by pretending the problem does not exist.

Your Church leadership finally surfaces the problem through an announcement in a congregational meeting. At that meeting, the pastor and board chairperson explain the crisis and how they plan to fix it. They tell those present that everything that has become tradition and routine through the years is subject to change. They will evaluate and decide which ministries to keep, examining the remaining ministries to discover how they might improve. They will protect only the foundational truths of the Bible.

People stare at the pastor and leaders with numbing disbelief. Slowly, over the next few weeks, people begin to realize the leaders are serious. The conclusion that rules the hearts of the members of Your Church is that anything the members find comfortable is likely to change.

Two prominent defensive behaviors surface: attack and avoid. Some members are afraid and attack. Others are afraid and avoid.

The attackers ask questions like "Who caused this crisis?" or "Whom should we fire?" or "Leadership is exaggerating and going too far." The avoiders will outwardly go on as if nothing has happened, avoiding the issue altogether. Both groups are afraid and not dealing with fear effectively.

Mildred has been teaching the six- and seven-year-old children on Sunday morning for ten years and loves it—even gets her identity from it. She fears that she may not be able to teach that group anymore. Moreover, she does not believe that she is able to start a new ministry. Life in the church looks uninviting for her, so she is afraid and pulls into her shell. Soon, she stops coming to church.

Frank has a similar problem, but his is with the adult Bible study. His class is not doing well, and he knows that something is wrong. The only people who attend his class are those who do not want to hurt his feelings. People have told Frank that his class is boring, but he is afraid to think of doing something else. With the congregational announcement, leadership is forcing Frank to deal with reality. He is frightened because he believes that he will lose the few loyal friends he has, and everyone will know the truth about him. Frank is angry and strikes out at the leaders.

Leaders see Mildred as a quiet person who does not cause problems, but do not notice that she has stopped coming. They see Frank as a fighter and complainer and would rather see him either change or leave. Both people are dealing with their personal fears.

Change Takes Time, and the Longer It Takes, the Harder It Is to Cope

Business mergers take time. For the staff, a year can go by from the merger announcement to the time the employee is in the new position or has found a new job.

However, church transition can be longer. Churches will struggle for several years trying to make a change without actually making a change. Church leaders will try a token change, which is a change that may be only one step of what would be a plan if they had a plan. They might shoot at a false target, such as attacking a symptom like poor attendance, rather than addressing what is causing the drop in attendance. They do not want to hear that the services are lifeless and dull, so they will form committees and subcommittees to look into a myriad of details. The progression can take years, so long that often the urgency of the original mandate from the board softens. Little or no actual change takes place. Eventually, the day the leaders predicted arrives, and the church shuts the doors for the final time. It is too late to save it.

Back during the attempt to change, most of the leaders and some of the members of the congregation recognized what was happening. They saw the hesitancy of the other leaders and the rest of the congregation as ploys to stop change. It was so frustrating. Can the people not see the end that will come if they do nothing? Can they not see that with the change, the church could return to the state of passion for God they used to experience? Do they not see how fun it would be once they made the leap from the edge of the pool into the arms of an adventurous yet tender and loving Father?

These frustrated leaders fail to identify the real enemy. It is not the people or the struggling leaders. It is the fear. Those who are attacking or hiding are the victims of their fear. The frustrated leaders finally reach the limit of their emotions and leave the church angrily. Those remaining feel a drop in tension and life returns to normal until the moment of the church death.

WHAT CAN LEADERS DO DIFFERENTLY?

To begin with, leaders can quit viewing people who are acting defensively (attacking or avoiding) as enemies. We can see them instead as the victims they are. Realize that helping scared, attacking, or avoiding people does not begin with an action, but with a theological shift in thinking.

Most people do not even know when fear is driving their behavior. But whether they know it or not, they need God's love poured out to them through us, the leaders. What the church does not need is us as leaders reacting to our attackers or avoiders with the same defensive behavior we are receiving. It is common for leaders to react defensively to the ones God has called them to love. When we view another person as an enemy, the tendency is for us to become defensive in return and attack or avoid that person. However, when leaders react defensively, the negative impact is greater than when members of the congregation act the same way.

God is calling churches to select special people to be leaders who do not react defensively to people who are attacking or avoiding them. The church needs for leaders to exhibit the fruit of the Spirit, especially during times of change and conflict. Notice that it is not "the fruit of training or study." The leadership patience needed to transition change in the church today is the fruit of a deep, lasting, dependent, and obedient love relationship with Jesus Christ. The church needs leaders who are living sacrifices, who allow God, and not their own fears, to be in control.

Why is it so critical for God to be in control? Because it is the only way to have the power necessary to do what God calls us to do. Jesus Christ did not work independently but said, "Don't you believe that I am in the Father, and that the Father is in me? The words I say to you are not just my own. Rather, it is the Father, living in me, who is doing his work" (John 14:10).

To help people through the fears they will experience when change occurs in their lives, you must view them as victims rather than as enemies. You need to see them as ministry fields rather than as problems. You need God working in you and through you to love consistently those who attack you. You need to be walking in the Spirit (Gal. 5).

Assuming we have allowed Jesus Christ to rule in our lives to the point that we are a living sacrifice in *every area* of our lives, then how can we help fearful people during change in the church? The following suggestions are a result of years of experience helping churches deal with change.

Expect a Fear Reaction (Attacking and Avoiding)

When we expect change to cause people to respond with a normal fear reaction, in the form of attacking or avoiding, we will discover that we will experience less emotion ourselves. Remember the mother in the pool with her son. If the mother had entered the pool expecting that she was going to ask her son to do something he had never done and that he would likely be afraid, as normal children will, she would have reacted differently. Think about when we are talking to a one-year-old baby. We do not get adult conversation in return, at least not with words. Yet we do not get upset. We expect the baby to act like a baby.

Therefore, when we lead change in our church, expect people to act normally—with a fear reaction in the form of attacking or avoiding. When we deal unemotionally with the fear of others, we will discover there are two kinds of attacking and two kinds of avoiding.

People who attack will either attack us or attack the change idea. The attack against us sounds something like "You are unfit!" The attack against the idea is more like "This is a dumb idea!" (Please do not confuse attack with normal and healthy dialogue.)

The avoiders are similar. One avoider will avoid us personally. He or she will see us coming down the hall and move out of our sight. The other avoider will be happy to see us but will change the subject whenever we bring up the issue of change.

Leaders prefer having avoiders in the church, since they do not set up confrontation. However, there is a big problem with avoiders. They leave leadership with the illusion that everything is moving along without a problem. The avoiders quietly slip into the background. Often leaders will label avoiders as "backsliders" because they appear to be moving backward in their church participation.

Leadership does not like attackers. They are in your face. They force us to deal with issues we would rather not deal with. They are labeled "rebellious." If not helped adequately, the attackers will finally quit and leave.

On the other hand, if we do not help the avoiders adequately, they will quit and stay. Eventually, your church will have plenty of avoiders in the background doing little in the church. Sound familiar?

Listen with a Loving Ear

Many leaders get far too much exercise "jumping to conclusions," assuming they already know everything they need to know without seeking any more information. When they do succeed in asking a question, they often stop with the first and usually most superficial answer. People protect themselves. They are seldom going to give us a deeply personal and well-thought-out answer, no matter how accurate it might be. They will not likely say something like "The reason I am attacking you is because I am afraid that I will be embarrassed in the new role I am going to have, if in fact, I have any role. If I do not have any role in the church after the change, I will be devastated because people will think that I am not competent. And of course, I will know they are correct because I have always felt inadequate."

People would not likely admit to that level of self-understanding even if they did have it. Instead, leaders and congregation will continue to pretend to deal with issues but seldom get to the heart of the matter.

Leaders must ask questions and listen carefully to the answers if we are going to discover what is happening in the life of an attacker or an avoider. When people respond to your question, they may give you a great deal of information, some of which is germane and some irrelevant. Your task is to ignore the statements that are irrelevant to the issues that you're trying to address, select the statements that are germane, and keep the conversation moving in the relevant direction. To be a selective listener, you have to concentrate on what the speaker is saying, resisting the temptation to think ahead about what your response will be.

Have Many Parties

If you leaders want to cut off all heartfelt discussion, then do this: Have a meeting to give people a chance to ask questions and express their thoughts. At that meeting, we may get a few attackers to shoot a few surface questions or comments at us. But we will seldom get the heart issues. There is a place for meetings, especially for sharing information and giving people the opportunity to ask *clarifying* questions. However, it is at parties that people begin to relax and speak from the heart. It is when people have some food in their stomachs and are feeling good that they become expressive. This is especially true when the questions are not interrogation, but caring conversation—when our eyes, facial expressions, and tone of voice communicate concern for them.

If leaders want to know the heart and pulse of the church, it is at the party they can discover the truth. However, it is hard work for a leader to go to a party if he wants to learn the heart of the church. A leader is not there to be witty, impressive, expressive, or important. A leader is at the party to be a loving servant opening himself or herself up to the heart of another person to learn. A party is never the place to sell a program or idea. It is always the place for leaders to listen to hearts.

Involve People in Small Steps

There is something about involvement that helps people feel like they are part of a group. Participation gives them a sense of belonging; it provides stability, identity, and comfort.

To help people with their fears, give them something to do that is small and safe, especially in groups; it will help them keep their association with the church. When people are active with others, they have less time to languish in their fear.

Do Not Push Too Fast—but Do Keep Pushing

During a change environment, if leaders push too hard, those pushed, especially those wrestling with fear, will suffer. Change is like pregnancy. Once the change begins, there is a gestation period before a healthy birth can take place. If the push for change is too hard, then premature birth can occur and there will be an unhealthy result.

On the other hand, not pushing enough can be equally devastating. People do not like to change. They will find many reasons to delay the project. There may be a few reasons for delay; but there are more reasons to proceed. Unless leadership keeps the pressure on, the change will die an unnatural death—death through neglect.

During the planning phase, we should put *as much* time and effort in planning to help people deal with their fears as we spend in planning the change itself. During the implementation of the change phase, including the announcement, we should put *more* time and effort into helping people with their fears than we do in other parts of managing the change.

Over the years, we have taken part in many change projects. We cannot recall one project where leadership did not adequately plan for the change. Yet we can recall some of those same change projects that were like bad surgery. The patient may have lived, but life would never be the same. The problems stemmed from a lack of planning of how leaders would help with people's fears.

Often leaders, even church leaders, judge themselves based on the change plan. Did the plan happen? Was the plan on time? Was the cost of the plan within budget?

But God has called church leaders to a higher standard. We have attempted to remind leaders what Jesus said in Matthew 22 when asked about God's greatest command. Jesus answered that it is to love God with all you are and to love others like yourself.

As leaders, we should ask ourselves the question, "If the project was a success from a worldly point of view but failed to love the affected people, would God be pleased?" Since God is concerned for his people and his church, leaders should be concerned about God's concern; there ought to be a carefully laid out plan to love the impacted people. That does not mean we should not make tough changes, but that we must love people through the process.

We will deal with implementation more thoroughly in chapter 15.

CHAPTER 10

MAKING TOUGH DECISIONS

Emotions typically run high when decisions made by the church affect you and your family. People really do care about those issues that touch their relationships, schedules, pocketbooks, or reputations. The church finds itself continually dealing with highly personal issues. This is how it should be. The church's foundation is Jesus Christ, but its building is people. People he died for. People God loves and calls his bride. When leaders make a decision that affects people, people desire to be a part of that process. They want their voices heard and their desires met.

Recently, I (Tim) experienced the passion our church has for growing godly relationships. Over the course of the past few years, we have been rediscovering the power of relationships—a journey that is transforming our lives.

In an information meeting, some new ideas were proposed for structuring our relationships. The idea of changing how we were organized to do ministry met with resistance. A healthy and passionate discussion broke out. A decision had to be made on the spot. What the leaders had planned for that evening was not unfolding, but there was energy flowing, and to stop the interaction would have quenched the Spirit. So, though not planned nor voted on, I made a decision to let the discussion flow. It was a tough call for me, because at that moment I felt the tension of "what had been announced" vs. "what was happening right now." For leaders in the church, making tough decisions is a daily experience.

MAKING TOUGH DECISIONS IS PERSONAL AND CORPORATE

Making tough decisions reminds us of our own personal struggles in becoming conformed to the image of Christ. God often deals with us in ways that we do not necessarily like. God's love never ceases, but he also never compromises his character. I am often reminded that the church is the bride of Christ. The work of God focuses on purifying his bride. The Word of God clearly and boldly states that God is preparing a holy bride for his Holy Son (Eph. 5:26).

Consequently, God's work involves all that would make the bride a more perfect and pure bride. Thus, change becomes the word of the day. Putting off our old sinful self and putting on the new self in Christ calls us each day to a life of obedience and change. This process often comes with reluctant surrender to our Lord. We often treasure those habits of the soul that make us feel comfortable in our earthly journey. Habits of self-indulgence, laziness, pride, addictions, and self-pity raise their voices in protest every time the Spirit of Christ calls for a life of surrender and self-sacrifice.

Our journey is not solitary. We travel with other pilgrims whom God calls us to love and serve. We are challenged by the audacity of the idea that we actually have to "get along" and live a life in unity with Christ and one another. Our sinful nature wishes everything could be about "me" and "mine," but there are others who call themselves followers of Jesus. We need to sing and worship the Lord together, yet we struggle with how, when, and where. Yes, it would be somewhat easier if we could decide on the "right" style of music, at the "right" time for worship, in the "right" kind of worship center, with the "right" worship leader. However, most of life in the church is not about what we would prefer. So how do we navigate the issue of making those decisions that would please our Lord and motivate his people to love and serve him?

Make no mistake about this leadership issue. *Leadership is about making biblically sound, Spirit-filled, wise decisions in a timely fashion.*

There was a commercial during the Super Bowl several years ago that demonstrates the challenge leaders face. It opened with a Western scene, cowboys astride their trusty steeds, dust filling the air, as the cowboys shouted and whistled to command the attention of those ... those cats? Yes, cats, not cows, were the objects of "them there catboys." Trying to get those independently minded, skittish cats to move in one direction at the same time was pretty much impossible. Yet, that is the challenge for church leaders today.

Today, as in any generation, God calls leaders to make wise biblical decisions that motivate the followers of Jesus to live well for our King. We want to challenge leaders to consider not only their style of leadership, but also the necessity of making decisions when the stakes are high and the pressure is great. We are confident most of those in leadership are seeking the Lord to discover his will for each situation. How is it, then, that we often find such differing answers to what decision the Lord is asking us to make?

Principle 1
Saturation with the Word and Prayer

What would a biblically sound process for making tough decisions look like? Let us look at a few biblical examples. The early church faced tough decisions from its very inception. Acts 1 begins not only with the reminder of Christ's commission to the church, but also answers the question "What do we do next?" Christ ascended and left the church behind. So the church gathered in prayer. That is an expected biblical answer, right? Of course. They were following a pattern that Jesus had taught them: Pray in private (Matt. 6:6), pray clearly and simply (Matt. 6:7–13), pray before the selection of disciples (Luke 6:12ff.), pray when you want others to understand you better (Luke 9:18), pray in the midst of death (John 11), and pray continually (Luke 11:9–10). So the church gathered, possibly out of fear of the Jews, but more significantly, I believe, out of obedience and faith to wait for what the Lord had promised.

During one of those times of prayer, Peter reminded them of Psalm 109:8: "may another take his place of leadership." This guidance from the Holy Spirit brought the church to ask God for an answer to a very difficult question—who would replace the betrayer? Who would fill the shoes of one selected by the Lord, yet who betrayed him? The church proposed two men. One was selected by the means of casting lots. The church said, "Lord, you know everyone's heart. Show us which of these two you have chosen" (Acts 1:24).

Casting lots is no longer a common practice. However, the central question is "Are we trusting God?" Whom are we trusting in as we make decisions? Whose will are we concerned about doing? Ours? God's? Fundamental to all wise decision making is the question "Whose will do we want to see accomplished?"

Praying and waiting on the Lord are easy to think about yet not necessarily easy to practice. We want action now. We need to get this done today. The world is spinning toward hell, and we need to do something about it now. Yet, the pattern of Scripture tells us to take time, possibly lots of time, to wait together on the Lord, and pray. What should we pray? What should the church be asking for as it prays about tough decisions?

Paul explains in 1 Corinthians 2:16, "But we have the mind of Christ." The point here is that through the Holy Spirit the very thoughts of God are communicated to the church in words that we can understand. Therefore, the Scriptures inform our knowledge of the will of God. So the Word of God, the Bible, must inform our prayers. It is God's self-revelation of his purposes and will. It will direct us toward how we should pray. How can we do this on a leadership level in the church?

A common contemporary experience that allows for an encounter with the living God, both individually and corporately, is seminars and conferences for the purposes of education. Many in the church have also been practicing retreats for the purposes of prayer and hearing the voice of the Lord. These experiences assume that God has spoken in his Word, but also that God speaks through his Word by his Spirit to the church today.

Although it seems like yesterday, it was more than twenty years ago that I (Tim) attended a leadership retreat with the leaders of the church I was then pastoring. We had been in a season of prayer, seeking the Lord together. The journey had been filled with bumps, turns, and unexpected halts along the way, but in those several days at the retreat we began to hear and see God's will unfold for us. Out of prayer, out of reading and meditating on God's Word, and out of countless conversations came a clear and energizing summary of God's plan for us. Bingo! We heard! We believed! We did!

Church leaders are called to make tough decisions for the church every day. How? First and foremost, we must devote ourselves to prayer, immersion in the Word of God, and listening to God.

PRINCIPLE 2
OBEY GOD, NOT MAN

The apostles, having received the baptism of the Holy Spirit, found a new boldness in preaching the good news of Jesus Christ. They passionately announced that Christ had risen, and in his name there was forgiveness of sins and the receiving of the Holy Spirit. This boldness brought persecution. The jealous Jewish leaders were threatened by the response of the people to the message they thought they had squashed by crucifying Jesus. Now there was a new outbreak of the preaching of Jesus as the Messiah. Preaching with boldness and miracles brought attention to the apostles. Bad attention! Arrests, trials, imprisonments, and beatings characterized the first few weeks after the birth of the church. The question of the day was "Will we obey God or men?" (Acts 4:18–20; 5:29).

We should make tough decisions out of obedience to God, not men. Whom are we trying to please? God or men? What pressures do we feel? Whom are we trying to impress? Tough decisions demand a clear understanding of what it is to obey God. The church's call to obedience puts us on the cutting edge of culture. The church is a catalyst that causes waves of reaction, upsetting many who want comfort and the status quo. Tough decisions may not always feel good, but the Holy Spirit brings faith, peace, and boldness to make them.

PRINCIPLE 3
THERE IS A COST TO MAKING GODLY DECISIONS

Tough decisions cost something. For the apostles, they cost imprisonment, harassment, and flogging. What was their response? "The apostles left the Sanhedrin, rejoicing because they had been counted worthy of suffering disgrace for the Name" (Acts 5:41).

What does this mean for those making tough leadership decisions today? First of all, it does not mean we live with a martyr complex. We do not need to go around thinking, *Woe is me, I am being harassed because of Jesus! No one likes me. I am just a lowly servant of Jesus.*

Second, we need to think sincerely about representing a true expression of Christianity. Are we culturally relevant or culturally compromised? Are we seeing true followers of Jesus Christ produced from our church or comfortable Christians? Are our lives being transformed by Christ or conformed to the world? Are we driven by success, significance, or sacrifice? Are we seeking to please others? Are we trying to satisfy our insatiable desire for personal satisfaction? Many tough questions arise as we think about obedience to Christ.

Third, what are we preaching and teaching as the good news of Jesus Christ? What is our message? What actions are we calling people to make? Do we "demand" anything from those who are followers of Jesus? Who is this Jesus that died for us, a wimp or the sovereign Lord? To please our Lord was the driving force in the lives of the apostles. Paul said, "We make it our goal to please him" (2 Cor. 5:9). And this greatest of goals is a costly one.

PRINCIPLE 4
LIFE OR DEATH?

Tough decisions mean life or death. Acts 5:1–11 illustrates the activity of the Holy Spirit in demonstrating his judgment on those who lie. The leaders of the church must affirm tough decisions by God on the people of God for their disobedience. Asking clear and crucial questions becomes the role of those leaders who model the filling of the Holy Spirit.

Tough decisions call for tough questions. Highly personal questions are the order of the day for the leaders of the church. The text of Scripture does not say how Peter knew that Ananias had lied. In Acts 5:3, Peter asks, "Ananias, how is it that Satan has so filled your heart that you have lied to the Holy Spirit and have kept for yourself some of the money you received for the land?"

That probably was not the easiest question to ask. Having just experienced many powerful expressions of the work of the Holy Spirit in and through his life, Peter may not have wanted to face again the work of the Evil One. He did not, however, ignore the issue. Peter asked the hard question, a highly personal question, and a question that confronted a life-and-death issue. Making tough decisions means asking the tough questions, which are honest with God, others, and ourselves.

PRINCIPLE 5
ENLIST OTHERS IN THE DECISION-MAKING PROCESS

The growth of the early church brought with it many problems. With these problems came the necessity to make strategic leadership decisions. The indwelling of the Holy Spirit most certainly was the divine guidance that we see in the activities of the apostles. Therefore, God's wisdom can be discerned through their behaviors. Acts 6 introduces the problem of racial discrimination. (We have not come far in the twenty centuries since, have we?) The apostles' response to this challenge instructs us in how to make quick and tough decisions.

First, they did not deny that there was a problem. Second, they listened well. They took time to hear the complaint. They did not make excuses. Moreover, they responded with a positive plan. They, as Moses of old, delegated the responsibility to competent people. "Brothers, choose seven men" (Acts 6:3). They believed in the work of God in and through others. The apostles understood their leadership role as prayer and ministry of the Word. They prevented distractions from their job and a distortion of their power. They multiplied the workforce through delegating the problem to competent people. Within a short time, the problem was addressed and solved. In addition, the work of the Lord continued unabated and without distractions or distortions.

Making tough decisions includes empowering others to be part of the answer. When we think too highly of ourselves, we distort the use of power. Leaders often make the mistake of assuming too much responsibility. God thinks in terms of team. The apostles addressed this highly emotional issue with the guidance of the Holy Spirit. And they allowed those with the problem to become part of the solution and in the process empowered competent leaders to serve the church.

We need to make tough decisions in light of who can be part of the solution, not the problem. When leadership releases power through proper identification and affirmation of others, tough decisions become opportunities for growth and development in the body of Christ. It is important not only *how* we solve problems, but also *through whom* we solve the problems.

PRINCIPLE 6
DELEGATION—A PATHWAY TO EMPOWERMENT

Delegation can go two ways—up or down the "hierarchy." In Acts 8, Philip, the evangelist, had experienced a phenomenal response from the people in Samaria. His preaching and the miracles God performed brought great joy to the city (Acts 8:8). Yet, the people had not received the Holy Spirit. So Peter and John came and laid hands on the new believers so that they would receive the gift of the Holy Spirit as promised by Jesus. This teamwork approach to the experience of salvation did not cause Philip to become jealous of Peter and John—he realized they were a team. Philip delegated to those above him, the apostles, to authenticate and complete the work of seeing the church born in Samaria.

Simon, the former sorcerer, wanted the power of the apostles for self-glory. Simon offered to buy this ability. Peter rebuked him directly. "May your money perish with you, because you thought you could buy the gift of God" (Acts 8:20). Philip understood, as Simon did not, that God has given gifts and roles to certain people that others do not have. The calling and gifts of God on each person's life need to inform our tough decisions. One cannot buy what only God can give.

In Acts 6, the apostles delegate a specific task to the seven deacons. They also delegate to the church the responsibility and criteria for choosing the seven men who will deal with the specific problem of resource distribution. So delegation can involve considering the specific criteria for personnel selection, the specific task, and the number of people to accomplish the task. Delegation then, whether up or down, should inform our decision-making process.

PRINCIPLE 7
THE ABSOLUTE ABSOLUTES

Acts 15 introduces how the church dealt with the tough issues of doctrine. Here the church confronts not just one person, as in Acts 8, but a group of individuals with a deep commitment to a value they held highly. The issue of salvation by faith in Christ alone was at stake in this debate and crucial decision. The context indicates that ethnicity also played a role in the disagreement. What would the apostles say? How would they handle this issue?

There were a number of witnesses to the truth of salvation by faith in Christ alone. Peter spoke up about the conversion of the Gentiles and that they had received the Holy Spirit. He emphasized that it was "through the grace of our Lord Jesus that we are saved, just as they are." Paul and Barnabas described how God had visited the Gentiles with miraculous signs and wonders. Then James concluded by quoting the prophet Amos, "and all the Gentiles who bear my name" (Acts 15:6–17).

Tough decisions, informed by the Word of God and multiple witnesses, bring clarity and unity to the church. All the apostles were saying the same thing. A united voice spoke for the church: the Word of God, the experience of seeing God bring the Gentiles to salvation as he had done with the Jews, and the evidence of signs and wonders. When there is consensus in the leadership of the church in concert with the Word of God, tough decisions can be made with confidence.

PRINCIPLE 8
EMOTIONS AND DECISION MAKING

Sometimes tough decisions are emotionally difficult to make. Paul and Barnabas ran into conflict about the value of John Mark as a fellow worker. Paul viewed John Mark as a quitter. Barnabas had sensed some growth and development in John Mark. So this dispute over a personnel issue led Paul and Barnabas to go in different directions (Acts 15:39). Tough decisions may not feel good, but can be good. Finding objectivity in emotionally charged issues requires that we submit our feelings to our thinking. There is a reason that labor negotiations have periods of "cooling off." In the same way, church leaders need to take the necessary time and space to gain a healthy view of the issues.

I often wonder why so many church boards, committees, task forces, etc., meet in the evening, even late into the evening, when people are tired and their energy levels are low. It seems we are asking for trouble. The Bible does say, "the spirit is willing, but the body is weak" (Matt. 26:41). Wisdom then calls us to plan and schedule meetings for ministry when the body and spirit can be in top form.

God also gives the members of his body different perspectives. Though Paul and Barnabas had a "sharp disagreement," the ministry went on. The Lord still used Barnabas and Paul. The expansion of the good news into Europe came as a result. John Mark matured under the mentoring of Barnabas, and years later Paul requested his ministry at a very crucial time (2 Tim. 4:11).

We need to be warned that emotions can distort and dominate decisions in an unhealthy way. Therefore, be sure to prepare well. Bad decisions are more destructive than no decisions. Working through tough decisions in the right way does not necessarily feel good. But bad decisions have complex outcomes. Therefore, allow the Spirit to control and fill every decision with his Word and his presence.

SUMMARY AND APPLICATION

Making biblically sound, Spirit-filled, wise decisions in a timely fashion is what leadership is mostly about. We can influence our churches for good when we apply these eight principles for making tough decisions. Saturation in the Word of God and intentional prayer heightens our ability to connect with God. This dynamic interaction with the Holy Spirit fills our minds and passions with his desires. In cooperation with other believers, this makes a vibrant community. Communities of the faithful dream of following God no matter what the cost. When testing comes that would draw them from this holy encounter, the church will have the courage to say, as Peter, "We must obey God, not men."

Churches with this vibrant nature understand there is a cost to being a true follower of Jesus Christ. Decisions that call for sacrifice give them a cause for which to live and die. Those with lesser passions find only a lukewarm experience with the living Christ. How sad to hear that some who call themselves by the name of our Savior have greedy intentions. Some who fellowship with the church are nothing more than spies and leeches, preying on the love and good nature of highly devoted believers. Jesus said that the kingdom of God is like a field where good and bad seed find root and grow together. Yet, at the end of the age, when the harvest comes, there will be a sifting. Followers of Jesus should not be distracted by those who follow the broad path.

When we choose to include others in the decision-making process, our trust inspires excellence. Trust generates energy for service and sacrifice. Therefore, we welcome the opportunity to see others as decision makers, not merely servants obeying our commands. There are times when we must draw the line in the sand. "No compromise here" should come from our lips when weaker minds or corrupted motives challenge the issues of orthodoxy. Think well and stand tall for the things that should never change.

Emotions turn black-and-white photos into living color. Without emotions, life would need no song. Yet our emotions can sometimes flood the boat and sink us. The Bible says that we are to take every thought captive to the obedience found in Christ (2 Cor. 10:5). Paul exhorts us to "submit to one another out of reverence for Christ" (Eph. 5:21). So our emotions and thinking need to find balance in submitting every feeling and thought to Christ and his church.

Tough decisions often require time and reflection. However, the process yields sound wisdom and fruitfulness for the church in fulfilling her mission for Christ.

SOME WILL STAY, SOME WILL GO

I (Tim) have two special friends from seminary days, Bob and Roger. We have now journeyed twenty-nine years since graduation day. We have served in numerous congregations in five states. We have discussed, pondered, and prayed over many relational issues. On a number of occasions we have struggled through knowing how to respond to folks who strongly disagree with us. From personal attacks on our character, calls, and/or giftedness related to the various options of ministry methods and programs, we have debated and dialogued about what we should do.

A common conversation keeps running through my mind over and over again. I think about the outcomes, "some will stay, some will go." Should we stay? Should we go? We cringe at the thought that our decisions or the decision of the board or congregation will influence some members to leave and seek another church. Or that in a parachurch organization, a decision to adopt a new style of ministry will cause some donors to stop giving, loyal staff members to leave, or board members to resign. Making tough decisions means "some will stay, and some will go." We must live by faith, even with tough decisions.

PART THREE

IMPLEMENTATION OF LEADING IN THE SPIRIT

CHAPTER 11

A PATHWAY FOR THE HOLY SPIRIT'S LEADERSHIP

Jesus said, "I will build my church, and the gates of Hades will not overcome it" (Matt. 16:18). What does that look like in the twenty-first century? We have had the privilege of traveling to scores of nations around the world in service to his church. It is easy to see that God loves variety. On many occasions, our experience has demonstrated that his church is dynamic, growing, and making a huge difference in our world. Churches, however, are not always healthy. Many churches experience a deviant form of Christianity. Nevertheless, God still works to heal and grow churches that reflect an intimate relationship with him and a caring ministry in their worlds, despite man's skewed approaches.

Up to this point, we have been challenged to consider the heart of the issue in church health and growth—are we intimately connecting with Jesus Christ? We believe the church has often neglected or not known how to be guided by the Holy Spirit. As Christian leaders, we need God desperately, and only in vital communion with him will we hear his voice and guide his people in holiness. This dynamic relationship between God and his people cannot be overlooked in our lives or ministries. In terms of leading a church or Christian organization, this relationship includes understanding the process of organizational leadership and management.

These ingredients and principles provide a healthy and productive way to see unity and fruitfulness in the body of Christ. Human effort cannot duplicate or replace the divine and supernatural. Yet the Holy Spirit has gifted many believers with leadership and management to lead and guide the church. As we think of what it means for the church to be Spirit driven, we cannot overlook those gifts of the Spirit given to his church for these purposes.

Christian A. Schwarz, in his book *Natural Church Development*, lists eight ingredients that contribute positively to growing a healthy church. One of the key ingredients in this growth process is the area of organization and administration. The church needs structure and process. The Holy Spirit has given certain believers these gifts. When administrative gifts combine with other ingredients, the church will grow. Therefore, Schwarz concludes, "a healthy environment causes churches to grow."[1]

You do not have to force them to grow—when the climate is right and the ingredients are well mixed, then the church naturally grows. Our life experiences have led us to write this book with an emphasis on the spiritual dimensions of leadership and management, and a view to connecting with God and living out his presence in all we do. Therefore, we have dealt with the need to walk by the power of the Holy Spirit and the process of listening to the voice of the Holy Spirit. The guidance of the Holy Spirit comes as we listen and obey.

Now we have arrived at the major reason for writing this book: organizational leadership and management led by the Holy Spirit. In our work with the church, we have experienced extreme reactions to the ideas of organization principles. Some say that these are principles of the world and should not be a part of leadership in the church. They prefer to look at the church only as relational and familial. These individuals lead the church as if it were a family, with very little emphasis on organizational principles. Others see the church as a business. These congregations are led by those who promote a great sense of accountability, goal setting, and structure. Many of these congregations have grown to be extremely large (mega churches) and are the preferred size of church for 12 percent of adults in America. In fact, at least 59 percent of all evangelical adults attend churches with over a hundred adult members. Americans seem to prefer bigness, options for worship times, focus groups (usually geared toward age or life stages), and especially ministry for children and youth. We are consumers, and our economy and church life often show it.[2]

Whether the congregation is twenty or twenty thousand, everyone deals with some form of organizational management. We submit to you that the principles and processes that follow, when united with a heart for God, a dependence upon him in prayer, and an expectation that he will meet with his church and empower her to grow, will be one of the most thrilling experiences of your life. We can think of nothing more exciting than to see a healthy local church or mission organization flourishing by the power of his Spirit and the leadership of his gifted saints.

We have observed congregations who have heard the voice of God as they sought him and dared to share their dreams together. They have found a unity of vision that propels them into a season of transformation and growth. Many churches have found this same experience. Maybe you long for such an experience, yet you are frustrated, not knowing how to lead your congregation through a proven process. Please read on. This proposed pathway can lead to health and growth for our church or Christian ministry. Anyone with courage, faith, and perseverance can find it as the Spirit of God leads. We believe it is worth our time and energy—and our lives.

WHAT IS THE SECRET?

The secret is when gifted leaders, relying upon the Holy Spirit, apply God-given principles of leadership and management in a systematic process. This results in supernatural growth. Growth that cannot be explained by our normal experience. God causes growth as we apply his truth to our church relationships. Growth and health will make the church attractive to those with no experience with the Lord Jesus Christ. Think with me as I walk through what this systematic process looks like.

STEP ONE: *Purpose*

Life has a purpose—God's purpose. God's purpose is that we know him and enjoy his presence so much that others identify us with him. We become divine agents of his life here on Earth. "Our lives are a fragrance presented by Christ to God. But this fragrance is perceived differently by those being saved and by those perishing. To those who are perishing we are a fearful smell of death and doom. But to those who are being saved we are a life-giving perfume" (2 Cor. 2:15–16 NLT).

STEP TWO: *Mission*

God's purpose for us is clarified in his mission for the church. Once Jesus was asked, "What is the greatest commandment?" He responded, 'Love the Lord your God with all your heart and with all your soul and with all your mind.' This is the first and greatest commandment. And the second is like it: 'Love your neighbor as yourself'" (Matt. 22:37–39). In his final days with his disciples, Jesus commissioned them with these words: "Therefore go and make disciples of all nations, baptizing them in the name of the Father and of the Son and of the Holy Spirit, and teaching them to obey everything I have commanded you" (Matt. 28:19–20). This mission has been the cry of the church for over two thousand years. Today billions of people on planet Earth know of his salvation and are followers of Jesus Christ. Many believers are diligently committed to knowing Christ and making him known. Make no mistake, Christ is building his church.

STEP THREE: *Vision*

Because the Holy Spirit lives in his church, unique callings of God are expressed in personal and corporate vision. Vision is highly personal. People have visions. The Spirit of God plants dreams in the minds and hearts of young and old.

One example was "Youth Alive 2005" in Beaverton, Oregon. This evangelistic endeavor brought over two thousand youths to the Sunset

High campus on April 30, 2005, to hear the message of the good news about Jesus Christ. This event was the culmination of a dream started some nine months earlier at a summer camp. The dream of one young man infected dozens of his classmates. Where did this dream come from? It came from God the Holy Spirit. How did it come? It came through the preaching of a gifted evangelist at a summer camp. What was the outcome of the dream? Hundreds of high school students heard the gospel of Jesus Christ and were challenged to follow him.

We need to understand the power and process of vision. Chapter 12 will lead us closer to that ability. God's mission needs personal and contemporary expressions. Therefore, God consistently speaks to his people about how to fulfill his mission in each generation. These visions may last for a short or long season. We feel that vision captures God's plan for a certain people for a season of life's journey. Vision or dreams need to be celebrated when fulfilled and renewed for the needs of each new generation.

Once vision captures your mind and heart, you need a pathway for carrying out the vision. If it is not developed, the dream will be only a passing fancy. However, when you embrace the God-ordered methods and processes for crafting your vision into a reality, you will know the power of God in a whole new dimension. The rest of this book will develop for you the steps of planning and organization. These principles reflect the nature of God as Creator. God is a designer. God is a team builder. God is a worker. "And I am sure that God, who began the good work within you, will continue his work until it is finally finished on that day when Christ Jesus comes back again" (Phil. 1:6 NLT).

STEP FOUR: Pray and Plan

God is working today. God is working in us. He also desires to work through us. How? God works through us by his Spirit, by his ordained principles of leadership and management, and by the gifted Christians that he empowers.

The church is composed of people. People create the team for ministry. People *are* the ministry. So with planning come people. Who has God brought together as a team? The team owns the dream when they are involved in praying and planning the action steps that will make the dream a reality. Therefore, the team should be strategically involved in praying and planning the strategies for fulfilling the dream.

STEP FIVE: Organization and Structure

Organization clarifies who is to do what, who is to work with whom, who is to report to whom, and when all of this should be done. Organization should create an environment where people feel safe and work productively. Why? As a God of order, Jesus wants his church to feel secure. He created the universe in an orderly fashion. "He sustains everything by the mighty power of his command" (Heb. 1:3). He used the apostles to organize the church (Titus 1:5). He commands that the church run in an orderly fashion (1 Cor. 14:40). God wants you to be happy. Happiness does not happen for long in a chaotic state. Structure and order bring peace and harmony into relationships. Form can become rigid and deadly, but when evaluation and renewal are regular parts of the leadership process, life is preserved for all involved.

Some churches are hyperorganized and minimize spontaneity and innovation. Other churches lack organization, and suffer from inefficiency and missed opportunities. Lack of organization creates an unsafe environment. Overorganization, though often creating a safe environment, minimizes the ability to connect with the now. Things take so long to process that the church soon exists for the church and not for the vision that gave her birth and inspiration.

STEP SIX: Implementation and Reporting

With the plan and people in place, ministry is implemented. Programs are designed and initiated. Money is raised and spent. Buildings are purchased and outfitted for services. Staff is hired.

Training sessions are conducted. Ministry of all shapes, sizes, and sounds begin to focus the church on serving our Lord.

STEP SEVEN: Evaluation and Renewal

Our lives are scarred by sin. We at best limp through life as wounded soldiers. Joy, however, is not dependent upon our condition, but our position in Christ. Therefore, everything we touch is in need of renewal. Our imperfections soon taint what we create. The ministries we create to serve others are often maintained to serve ourselves. The church cries out for renewal. The Spirit of Christ within us longs to be fresh and relevant to the issues of our day, but sin keeps building calluses on our hearts and hands. What we create today in terms of ministries for the church needs review and renewing tomorrow. This is the condition of our fallen world.

Therefore, church leaders must consistently evaluate and modify their plans and programs. Why? Because we are sinners and need God's grace in all we do. We must check motives and methods in order to remain holy and useful. He is sacred. We are sinners. God's absolutes empower us to analyze all that we are and do. When we are judged and disciplined by the Lord, we will NOT be condemned with the world (1 Cor. 11:32).

Organizational leadership and management principles, when applied to the church, inspire people to excel in ministry. When people have a compelling vision, a clear pathway of service, a team with the same vision, a coach to clarify questions, and the Holy Spirit living within, supernatural things happen. Leaders do need to follow the ways of God in ministry. Methods are not sacred, but God does use them. Only the power of God can cause supernatural things to happen. Yet God does work through people to make them happen. The Spirit of God came upon the church in Acts 2 in a supernatural way. Yet, from that moment on, he came only through the preaching of the gospel and the laying on of hands by the apostles. God works through people, not in spite of people. Therefore, we call upon you to gain a new boldness and confidence in God and his ways with us.

FULFILLING THE VISION

Do you have a dream? Is there something you believe that God wants you to do? Are you constantly under the influence of God? Do you have a burning passion that he is calling you to serve him in a certain way? What are you going to do about it?

To do nothing about a dream or vision is to allow the fire to cool and the wind of indifference to chill our souls. Instead of indifference, faith says, "Make a plan!" Faith says, "What's the next step?" Faith says, "Whom can I connect with?" and "Who has done this before?" and "Where are others doing something like this?"

Do you have a plan and no team? Do you have a team and no resources? Has your ministry run dry and there is no power? Is your church living on past memories? Do you need a touch of God? We believe that you can be renewed in your walk with and service for God. But today you need to act. You need to take one step in the direction of obedience to him. God is reaching out to you! You need to return the favor and reach up to him! How?

Commit your life to an utter dependence upon the Holy Spirit. God will speak to you and your church today. Show your faith with a pen and paper (or computer if you like). As we read and answer the questions raised in chapters 11–16, write down your thoughts. We believe these are thoughts from the Holy Spirit of God to your spirit. God has a vision, plan, and team for you to lead or be a part of for the purposes of his kingdom. Don't miss the opportunity to worship and serve the King of Kings and Lord of Lords!

After you have written your notes, take time to meditate with the Holy Spirit. Then, retitle your notes and set a prayer agenda. Begin a dialogue with God. Ask him, "Where's the team? When should we start? Where should we begin?" Or, "How do I start over? Whom do I need to be reconciled with?"

We will now work through these concepts and complete a chart[3] on these topics in subsequent chapters and the readers' guide as we discover God's intentions for the church. See the appendix for more information.

CHAPTER 12

WHAT GOD HAS IN MIND: PURPOSE, MISSION, AND VISION

I ntimacy—open and transparent intimacy—is the desire of millions of hearts today. Real intimacy is that elusive, indescribable relationship that seems just out of reach, similar to the pot of gold at the end of the rainbow. Yet our Father God is offering that intimacy with him, an affectionate relationship so deep that it overwhelms every part of us, drawing us deeper into him. This is what we have been laying before you, specifically as it relates to the church and church leadership.

Throughout the book, we have attempted to paint the picture that leadership flows out of a deep, dynamic, dependent love relationship with Jesus Christ. We have described how our relationship with Christ drives our hearing (chapter 5), our love for people (chapter 6), our understanding of his guidance (chapter 7), our understanding the impact of fear on leadership (chapter 8), our ability to help others with their fear (chapter 9), and how we make tough decisions (chapter 10).

All of this is important, yet in an organization such as a church or a parachurch ministry, what we do tomorrow morning when we get up starts with purpose, mission, and vision—and that also comes from God.

DEFINE YOUR TERMS

There is confusion over what purpose, mission, and vision mean. For example, two of our favorite authors, Aubrey Malphurs and Bobb Biehl, differ on purpose and mission. Malphurs separates purpose and mission. He says that "purpose answers the question about why we exist, while mission answers the question about what we are supposed to be doing."[1] Biehl considers the purpose statement and the mission statement the same. The mission (purpose) statement answers the question "Why does our team exist?"[2] Both authors agree on the initial question, but Malphurs separates mission from purpose. The point is that both men are highly regarded and credible men in the same field, yet both have different uses of words to discuss similar concepts.

There is only one way we know of to deal with confusion within your church leadership. You are going to have to spend the time clarifying and agreeing on words and their definitions. What we should not do is enter into discussion having differing definitions for our words. It would be like a family conversation where the father is commenting on the number of aliens in the city (thinking "people who are not citizens"), and the child is commenting on how he or she would like to meet one (thinking "beings from another planet").

Unfortunately, the confusion over words and definitions is all too common, and even more unfortunate is that leaders are unaware of the confusion, since most assume that their own words and definitions are common to everyone. The result can be misunderstanding or conflict or both.

In order to minimize confusion in this chapter and to be able to center on implications, we will provide a common basis for discussion by providing our definitions for the terms we use.

Purpose Statement

We draw from both Malphurs and Biehl for the opening thought—God's purpose for our church or ministry. The purpose statement answers the question "Why do we exist?" That is a difficult question to answer. It is certainly fraught with theological implications.

If we assume that God created the world primarily to demonstrate his power, then our answer would be in light of that. If we assume that God created it to focus attention on himself, then our answer would be in light of that. If we assume that God created us out of an outpouring of the infinite love within the Trinity, then our answer would be in light of that. If we hold all three assumptions, and possibly more, then our answer to the question "Why do we exist?" would be in light of all our assumptions. A study of the names of God may be a helpful exercise to uncover our assumptions and with that why we exist. The question about purpose is not an easy question to answer, and not one we individually will answer quickly. Corporately, it will take even longer, since it involves wrestling over assumptions and implications with many people. Yet it is important.

It is important to write our purpose statement and keep it before our leadership and congregation continuously to prevent a distraction from God's purpose for us. Leaders (including great leaders) can get so busy doing ministry that they forget why they exist.

Mission Statement

Again drawing from Malphurs, and to avoid confusion over words, the mission statement as we use it asks the question "What are we supposed to be doing, or what is our divine, strategic intent?" It will take a great deal of prayerful discussion by leadership before we come to a point of agreement and then write God's mission statement for our church.

We have read many different mission statements and most draw from the Great Commandment to love God and to love others (Matt. 22:37–40), or the Great Commission to go and make disciples (Matt. 28:19–20), or both.

IMPORTANCE OF THE PURPOSE STATEMENT
AND THE MISSION STATEMENT

Why is it important to know and often recall God's purpose and mission for our congregation?

God's purpose and mission for our congregation is the standard of decision making—including how to spend God's money and where to focus the time and energy God is giving us. There are two distinct issues we as leaders face continuously.

First, there are so many good ministries to do for God. The problem is that some of those ministries may not be what God wants us to do. They may be good but they may not be God's best. There will always be competition for our attention.

Unfortunately, it is not always easy to separate the good from the best. A member with influence wants to start a ministry, a good ministry that the member has wanted to do for years. Do we as leaders let them do it? It seems like a good ministry, so why not? Because that new ministry may not be what God wants done. It may not fit into God's purpose and mission for our church. Purpose and mission provide a scale for evaluation more reliable than personal opinions.

Second, living in urgency has become normal for leaders. Yet much of what we call urgent may not be important. In a family, it can be so urgent to watch a particular television program or sporting event that we ignore our children or spouses, who are more important. In a church, we can allow urgent but not necessarily important programming to usurp God's important ministry of loving and growing people.

It is easy to put off what is important. "I will spend more time with God as soon as I get caught up with my work." "As soon as I get my promotion and an increase in salary, we will start giving to God." "I will invite the neighbors over for a meal to get better acquainted as soon as I finish the yard work." "We will start an evangelism thrust in our church as soon as we can afford to hire someone to lead it."

It is not always easy to separate the urgent from the important. God's purpose and mission for our church provides a scale to evaluate what is important. Measuring against God's purpose and mission is central to making "what is best or important" decisions.

It is difficult to evaluate anything from God's view, let alone remember God's purpose and mission when self-interest is clouding our view. Think honestly for a moment about how many decisions we make without consciously considering God's purpose and mission. Think about how many ministry decisions are made because of concern about things other than God, such as fear of what people would say. It is a normal, real struggle—a struggle godly people have. Naturally, pride wants people to pretend the struggle does not exist.

Just knowing God's purpose and mission for our church is not enough. Purpose and mission *must be the standard* of all ministry evaluation. Leadership must remain constantly vigilant, guarding against making decisions based on anything other than God's purpose and mission.

INGREDIENTS OF A VISION STATEMENT

Vision is an extremely difficult word to put into a concise definition, or to ask with a simple question, but let us try with this question: "What is the clear, unique, and inspiring word picture of the ministry God intends for you for a period of time, which will be consistent with his purpose and mission?" To develop this definition, we are providing what we believe are the key ingredients of a vision.

1. A Vision Comes from God

In the New Testament, the word "vision" is used for some form of communication from God, such as when God told Ananias through a vision to go pray for Saul (Acts 9:10–12). There was also the time that Cornelius had a vision when an angel of God visited him (Acts 10:3). Then there was Peter's vision in Joppa (Acts 11:5). In the New Testament visions came from God and he told someone to do something.

Today believers say things like "I believe God has given me a vision for the lost," or to go to a particular country. Other people have been reading the Bible and sensed God was leading them to do whatever it was they were reading. In many ways, when a Christian reads the Bible and gets a real sense from God that he or she should stop doing something that is wrong, or start doing something for God, that person is receiving a vision from God. It might not be as dramatic as Peter's vision, but it is just as much a specific directive from God. A major tenant of the Christian faith is that God communicates to us through his Word. Although it may not be a dream, an angel, or a voice, it is still God communicating with us.

The beautiful thing about vision is that we can check a vision against Scripture to see if it in any way disagrees with what it says. The implication is that the vision we or our church follows ought to be the one that God has given.

2. A Vision Is Uniquely Ours (Church, Ministry, or Individual)

In each of the visions written in Acts, the vision was unique for one person or a group of people. It was unique to Ananias, Cornelius, and Peter. It was unique to Paul, Luke, Silas, and Timothy when the Spirit called them to Macedonia and prevented them from going to Bithynia. Paul had been the one to see the vision, but it was uniquely meant for all of them to do one thing and *not* to do another thing. That does not mean that other people or groups might not be called to Macedonia, but it does mean that on that day and place, the call was uniquely for them.

There are two implications about how our church chooses ministry direction. In her book *When the Soul Listens*, Jan Johnson quotes pastor and author Peter Lord:

> When God has blessed others by using certain methods, we sometimes presume that we should use those same methods. We don't realize that God blessed that way for others because that's the way he ordered them to do things.

> Nowhere is this more common than in church programs. One church prays and receives an answer—a specific method of carrying out a certain order of God. They are richly blessed because God blesses what God orders. Then another church, seeing this blessing, copies the program— because they believe God is blessing the program itself. They fail to realize that what he is really blessing is *obedience*. And they never stop to ask him, "Father, what do you want us to do?"[3]

Please do not shortcut the time of prayer, study, and discussion and simply settle for what some other church has done (unless you have been given the same vision after your time of prayer, study, and discussion).

The second implication is that we as individuals or our team will be hearing from God from time to time about what it is he wants us to do or stop doing, as the case may be. We state that last sentence emphatically. We both believe that a significant reason many churches flourish is because they stay sensitive to God's dynamic and unique leading.

3. A Vision Needs to Be Clear and Provide Direction

In each case where vision is mentioned in Acts, the vision became clear to the recipient, and God provided specific direction. The examples in Acts reflect the time following Pentecost, when the Holy Spirit had begun his new work.

Since that time and throughout the centuries, God has been providing vision to his saints, leading them with clear and specific direction. God was leading Paul as he traveled throughout Asia and Europe. God has been providing missionaries with the vision to go to all parts of the world to share the good news. Most of us who are reading this book are in leadership roles because God gave us the vision to do it.

As you write your vision statement, be sure that it is clear, that it is easily understood, that it uses words that are not ambiguous or jargon. The goal is not a statement that is clever or alliterates well. The goal is clarity.

Also, as you write your vision statement, be sure that it provides words that give direction to your church, not just words that are clichés or high-sounding intentions.

4. A Vision Will Provide Energy and Be Inspiring

I (Allen) can testify that nothing gets me as fired up, energetic, and inspired as stepping into something that God has given my wife and me a vision for. Mary and I left our careers and stepped into trusting God day to day for not only our cash flow, but also what he has had us to do. Mary and I decided that we were not going to force ourselves into (or even accept) a specific ministry if God did not give us the vision for it.

Since that time, it has been one thing after another. We had the vision that God wanted us to attend seminary, which we did. We believed God wanted us to move back to Olympia to start a planned giving program in a church, to help a number of churches with budgeting and other financial-management issues, and to help my father in the last months of his life, all of which we did. All the rest of the ministries in which Mary and I are involved, including this book, are ministries we did not come up with on our own, though they are consistent with our dreams.

I mention dreams. As a side note, I believe that most Christians today are afraid of dreams. I do not mean the dreams you have when you sleep, though I do not discount them. When I say dreams, I mean what it is that you enjoy so much that you would choose it if the choice were left totally up to you. Tim and I believe that God's vision for us is something we would choose, if we had all of God's information and perception. We have had the privilege of living out the dreams God has given us. And many of us have the same testimony. Hasn't it been inspiring?

5. A Vision Is for a Season (Project, Day, Month, Year, Decade, or Many Decades)

The shortest vision I (Allen) ever had was the vision to help two men intending to do evangelism and education in Africa. They needed someone to come alongside to help them put together a business plan so their organization could be approved for a 501(c)3 nonprofit status. That one only lasted about a month. But God's vision for them in Africa will likely last for decades.

6. A Vision Is Important (Prevents Distraction by Unimportant Things)

Like purpose and mission, vision acts as a standard to measure choices of things to do with money and time. There will always be competition for the money and time that God entrusts to us.

If God has given our church the vision to reach the students of a nearby university, then God will be expecting us to put a great deal of the church budget and ministry time of the congregation and leaders into reaching those students. If another ministry opportunity comes along, one that God has not placed on the heart of our church, and we remember the vision God gave us for this current season, we will have no difficulty saying no.

AN OLD TESTAMENT VISION

In Joshua 1, God gave Joshua a great short-term vision—defeat Jericho. The Lord reminded Joshua that he was about to give the Israelites this land and stirred them to get ready to receive his gift. God described even the specifics of what it was they would be receiving and how nobody could stand against them. God reminded Israel that he would be with them all the way. What inspiring words to get them energized. Then God told them he was going to amaze them and would bring Joshua glory—another word picture to inspire them.

After they crossed the Jordan, God provided more of the vision. God was going to give Jericho into Israel's hands, including the king and all the warriors. Would we not like to know in advance that God was going to give us victory in the battle we were about to fight for him? Would that not inspire us?

There are some interesting observations to make about the vision of defeating Jericho.

First, God did not reveal the specific Jericho vision until it was time to act on it. And then he revealed only a piece of the vision at a time. It would seem that God does not need to keep his children informed far in advance of what he intends for us. We might conclude that he intends to keep us a little bit in the dark. We could draw the implication that God wants his children to trust him and to live with faith on a day-to-day basis. Our pastor, Matt Hannan, compared Joshua's taking the Promised Land with the development of the Christian life, a life filled with surprising adventures (vision).

The second observation about the vision of taking Jericho is the difficulty or even impossibility of the vision. Jericho was a seemingly impenetrable fortress. Surely, there was an easier first city. This cannot be what God wanted. Wait until we get to chapter 13, when we address the unbelievable plan God gave Joshua on how to defeat Jericho. But for now, the vision of defeating Jericho is overwhelming enough.

I (Allen) recently returned from teaching in a church in a small city in Ukraine. This church has been receiving aid from churches in other countries. I asked the pastor what he would say if God were to give him the vision that within five years that church would no longer need any outside support and in fact would be supporting its own missionary in another city in Ukraine. The pastor said, "Wow! That would be a Jericho to us."

Why should leaders today not embrace Jericho visions? I wonder how often God intends for his churches to have a Jericho vision, but it never happens because leaders keep the right to make the final decision because fear rules in their hearts (review chapter 8).

What is it that drives church leaders to recoil when facing a Jericho vision? It could be any number of causes.

Fear is a paralyzing emotion. Lack of trust in God limits our view of our true resources. Lack of support from other members of the congregation isolates us at the time we most need interdependence. Conflict in the congregation destroys our motivation to go the extra mile. Modern rationalism erodes the faith needed to step forward into a greater vision.

We might fail with a Jericho vision, but, perhaps, it would be worth it.

EVALUATION TIME

What are we doing in our church? Are we in a safe church, safe because we are never stretched to a Jericho vision?

It may be time for us leaders to have some scary yet honest discussions about why our church exists. We may need to get into Scripture and into serious prayer and discover God's purpose and mission again. We may need to take a hard look at the needs of our community, both physical and spiritual, and embrace a Jericho vision.

I have heard it said that all churches have a Jericho, something challenging, even scary, that God has placed on the hearts of the leaders. If we already know what our Jericho is, the only question that remains is "What will we do about it?"

The common thread through this chapter and the entire book is the leader's dependent love relationship with Jesus Christ at the center of leadership and the recognition of Christ's sovereignty in all matters of his church and our individual lives. Leading the church in the light of God's purpose, mission, and his vision for our church is no different. Leadership's obedience to the purpose, mission, and vision is to flow out of that love relationship, an intimacy with Christ that grows from a daily walk with him.

THE VISION AND THE PLAN

The *vision* and the *plan* are two sides of the same coin.[4] (The coin is the community of people in a dynamic relationship with Christ.) We addressed the vision in this chapter. The *plan*, which we will cover in chapter 13, asks, "What are the specific measurable steps needed near term to accomplish this vision within the context of God's purpose and mission through and in us?"

PLANNING

For thirty-five years in banking, I (Allen) labored under the hammer of the business plan. Every fall the business plan became the center of our focus, and for good reason. The plan was the standard by which we were measured the following year. If you were too aggressive with your plan, then you had to live with it for the whole year; so you did not want to be too confident. On the other hand, if you were too conservative with your plan, there was always the chance that bank management would help you set a more aggressive plan; more aggressive than you would do for yourself.

The business plan included what you or your team projected to be your sales (vision), what you intended to do to reach your projected sales (plan of action), and how much it would cost to execute your plan (budget). The purpose of the business plan is to put structure to the process of achieving the purposes and mission of the organization.

INGREDIENTS OF A MINISTRY PLAN

A church plan or ministry plan is similar to the bank business plan in philosophy. It includes a word statement of what God intends for us to do for the next period of time (vision—discussed in the previous chapter), the actual steps we are going to take and what will be the results of those steps (plan), and how much it will cost to carry out the plan (budget).

As we described in chapter 12, if we had a coin with one side labeled "The Vision of the Church," the other side would be labeled "The Plan." In a sense, the plan and the vision are complementary, except the vision is made of words that are meant to inspire, to motivate, to educate, and to focus our congregation. The plan is the vision stated in ways that direct action, influence behavior, provide some sense of objectivity, and provide a basis of evaluating results. As stated at the end of chapter 12, the plan asks, "What are the specific measurable steps needed near term to accomplish this vision within the context of God's purpose and mission through and in us?"

The plan has the six ingredients listed in chapter 12 in common with the vision. Through the following, please keep in mind that all we have presented about the love of God, the command to love God, and the command to love others must be evident in any plan that is developed or implemented.

1. The Plan Comes from God

If the plan is based on the vision and the vision is from God, then the plan is God's plan. The plan will include specific steps that will allow for the overarching call of God to love others. The plan will accommodate the two roles of leaders: (1) to be a steward for Jesus Christ to lead his church where he directs them to lead it (God's vision), and (2) to be Christ's steward, to serve, love, and develop those same people the leader is leading (love for others), and to keep both roles in balance. The plan will also provide for the fear of other leaders and the fear of those being led. The plan will be developed by leaders whose affection for Christ, rather than for themselves, is the driving affection in their lives.

The plan and its development centers on the dynamic love relationship with Jesus Christ and all that relationship implies.

2. The Plan Is Uniquely Ours

Since the vision is uniquely ours, and the plan is the actionable steps we will be taking to accomplish the vision, the plan will be uniquely ours. Ours individually, as a church, or as a ministry. Jan Johnson's quote of pastor and author Peter Lord applies here as it did in the section on vision.

3. The Plan Needs to Be Clear and Provide Direction

As the vision statement provides clear direction about what God is leading us to do or where he is leading us to go, the plan does the same thing, only worded in measurable steps. For a plan to be helpful, it must provide people with the information about the specific actions they will be taking. The steps need to be worded in such a way that we are able to know when each step starts and when each step is completed. Otherwise the steps are only intentions.

4. The Plan Will Provide Energy and Is Measurable

It is difficult to be excited about accomplishing something when we do not know specifically what we will be actually doing. In fact, if we don't know specifically what we will be doing, we will likely be nervous about it. The plan provides that information. As a result, the plan will lower tension, minimize confusion, help leaders coordinate people, and put traction to the vision. A vision without a plan remains only a vision, interesting but accomplishing nothing.

Since the plan is measurable, it will help leadership keep the vision on track.

5. The Plan Is for a Season

One of the beautiful things about a plan is that it is for a specific period. If you purchase planning software, you will notice that it lays out a calendar upon which you build your plan. Planning is by definition time oriented and, therefore, for a season.

Your plan can be for a short-term vision such as a project. The plan can be for a year, several years, and even for decades. (Although for a plan that lasts decades, we recommend breaking that plan into shorter increments.)

6. The Plan Is Important (Provides an Objective Measurement of the Subject Vision)

The vision statement is subjective. You cannot know specifically when you begin or finish the vision. That is one of the powerful purposes of the plan. Because the plan is objectively worded into steps, it provides an objective measurement of the subjective vision. It allows leaders and managers something concrete to follow.

When the vision is God's vision for us, then the plan, with God's leading, will be God's plan and the budget (which is part of the plan) will be God's budget. This is important to remember through all the planning. After all, we are stewards for God.

PARTS OF A PLAN

The plan has three parts:

    A. The measurable steps needed to carry out God's vision, including goals.

    B. The manner in which we will handle the fears (reluctance) of the people in order that the vision can be successfully completed, all carried out within the context of love and unity as led by the Holy Spirit. (This is addressed in chapter 15.)

    C. The expected costs (the budget), which we address as an overview later in this chapter.

ALL CHURCHES PLAN

All churches plan. That is a bold statement. We say to ourselves that this is not true, because our church has no plan. Every year it is just business as usual. However, read on and let us make the case that all churches plan.

One church—let us call it ABC Church—used a simple process to create a unique plan for themselves. This church wanted to assure that their plan was based on God's vision for them and not just business as usual. So each ministry head of ABC was required to present a vision and plan for the coming year in writing and in person to the board. They were to pay special attention to the changes in direction from the previous year and explain why the changes were recommended. During the in-person presentation, which accompanied the written presentation, the board was able to ask questions to assure that they understood the vision and plan of the ministry head. They were also able to adjust the vision and plan if it strayed from the purpose and mission of the church.

Once the vision and plan were agreed upon by all the ministry directors, the financial side was addressed. Each ministry director gave a forecast of total ministry costs for next year based on the vision and plan. Once the board finalized the annual budget, the directors were asked to spread the annual numbers out over the twelve months of the year, based on their plan. ABC ended up with a vision, plan, and budget that agreed.

You probably realize as we do that not all churches plan that way. In fact, very few of the churches we have visited follow the method of ABC, except those that are required to follow denominational guidelines. The chart on the following page places churches into groups based on our estimate of the relative size of each group.

Sadly, we believe groups A and B comprise most of the churches that are in decline or on a plateau.

Remember the discussion on vision in chapter 12? We read about God giving Joshua and Israel the vision of taking Jericho and what

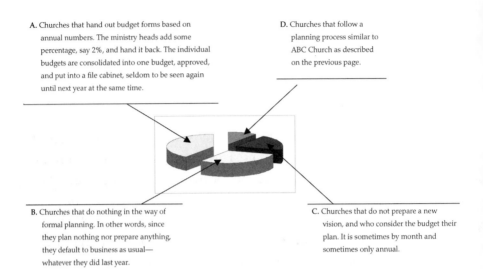

A. Churches that hand out budget forms based on annual numbers. The ministry heads add some percentage, say 2%, and hand it back. The individual budgets are consolidated into one budget, approved, and put into a file cabinet, seldom to be seen again until next year at the same time.

D. Churches that follow a planning process similar to ABC Church as described on the previous page.

B. Churches that do nothing in the way of formal planning. In other words, since they plan nothing nor prepare anything, they default to business as usual—whatever they did last year.

C. Churches that do not prepare a new vision, and who consider the budget their plan. It is sometimes by month and sometimes only annual.

an inspiring vision it was. By now, you may have been thinking about what kind of Jericho vision God might have for you or your church or both. Jericho was an enormous vision. However, please remember that God also gave Joshua a detailed plan to defeat Jericho. The principles we can pick up from this plan could shake our churches to the core.

THE PLAN TO DEFEAT JERICHO (JOSHUA 1–6)

God gave Joshua and Israel specific directions to defeat Jericho in two categories. First, he gave them measurable tasks to complete. God's instructions included when they were to start doing each task and when they had completed each task. Some of those tasks God gave them in advance, and other tasks he gave them at the time they were to perform them. Second, he directed them on how to deal with the emotions of the leaders and people.

Soon after Moses died, God began revealing his plan for Israel to move toward his mission for them, to inherit the land he had promised to them. As we pointed out in chapter 12, God directed Israel toward his first vision for them—to defeat Jericho. Little did Israel know how much God would be teaching them as he launched his plan to defeat Jericho.

What God did first was to tell Joshua to let Israel know the time had finally come to enter the Promised Land. They were to get ready by organizing all the material they would need for whatever might arise in their taking of the land. It took material to shelter, feed, and care for all the people of Israel. It may be surprising that God would address material as his first concern, but that is exactly what God did (Josh. 1:2–11).

In our own church, it takes money, supplies, facilities, equipment, people, and time to perform what God has called us to perform while caring for his people's needs. It may not be a very inspiring subject to address, but it is important to God.

As Israel traveled north on the east side of the Dead Sea and then to the Jordan River, they defeated the kings. As a result, Moses gave the land to the Reubenites, the Gadites, and the half tribe of Manasseh. Now that Joshua was in charge, he had a potential problem. There were forty thousand warriors in those two and a half tribes that were needed for the greater and longer-term conflict.

Therefore, the next step in God's resource plan was to assure that those warriors went with the remaining tribes as added military strength. It is significant to note that it was not just people God wanted from those two and a half tribes. God wanted the right people—the warriors (v. 12).

It is interesting how God's next step was about the right people; not just people but the right people, the warriors. We may not have enough of the right people in our church to carry out the vision and plan we believe God has for us. We should not despair. We may need to get serious about developing people to be the right people as an added step in God's plan for us.

Principle 1: *It takes organized resources, both materials and people, to carry out God's vision and plan for our church.*

PREPARING FOR OBSTACLES

Once Israel had organized the material and ensured that they had the right people to carry out God's vision and plan, Joshua put his focus on learning what Israel would face when they got to the other side of the Jordan. Joshua, an experienced surveyor of enemy territory, knew how to find out; he sent spies to evaluate and report to him about Jericho and the surrounding area.

Notice that Joshua did not send twelve spies. Maybe he learned from forty years ago that many spies do not guarantee accurate information. Joshua sent only two spies. We can imagine what information he needed. He would have wanted to know about evidence of strength, potential war material, defenses, and the heart of the enemy. The heart of the enemy was exactly what he heard about from the spies. The people were afraid of Israel (Josh. 2).

Once Joshua and the other leaders understood the obstacles that were ahead of them, they took the first step forward by traveling to the first obstacle, the Jordan River.

The Jordan River would seem to be an insurmountable obstacle. It would be one task to get warriors across, but an entirely different difficulty to get women and children across. Yet here they were, facing this overwhelming obstacle.

While we have seen churches doing their own vision and expecting God to come through for them as if he were committed to them, ignoring his own vision for them, we have also seen churches facing all kinds of insurmountable obstacles and have seen those obstacles topple. It has happened in my wife's life and my own.

Many years ago, I (Allen), my wife, Mary, and five other couples were convinced that God wanted us to start a Christian school in our community. We had a church that was willing to be the sponsoring church, but to start that fall, we had to have at least twenty students, teachers, and an approved and acceptable building by July 15—and the church could provide nothing but their name. It was already May—so we prayed for a miracle. We decided that first God wanted us to take the step of courage and make a significant sacrifice for God. We all put our entire savings into the project and prayed.

Within two weeks, we had received information about a couple in another town, both teachers, who were looking for positions in a Christian school. They were perfect, so we hired them. The following week we received a call from the superintendent of the public schools in our community who had heard from another source about our need. He offered us one wing of a closed school for just the cost of maintaining the building. He believed the public schools needed competition to keep them sharp. On July 14, we enrolled our twentieth student. When we opened two months later, we had thirty-five students and the experience of witnessing a miracle not unlike Israel crossing the Jordan. As a side note, that school has been ministering to children now for over thirty years.

Principle 2: *Facing an obstacle with God at our side opens the door to creativity and miracles.*

DEPENDENCE ON GOD

Israel was camped beside the Jordan River, preparing to cross. God was about to show Israel a mighty display of his creative miracles. Notice, there were specific and detailed directions about how they were to cross (Josh. 3:2–4).

It is easy to take shortcuts or ignore the concerns of God's people when leadership gets into the fray of day-to-day struggles. For Joshua, the immediate goal was to get all the people across the Jordan without losing or hurting one of them, yet do it God's way. It is the same for us as leaders. Our goal is to get through the obstacles without losing or hurting one person and to do it God's way. Who said being a leader is easy?

The last step Joshua took before taking Israel across the Jordan was to command people to examine themselves carefully for anything unclean, anything that they were attached to that stood between them and their love relationship with God. Was there anything they had affection for that was greater than their affection for God? This was the source of problems for Israel in the past and would continue through the time of Christ (v. 5).

Principle 3: *God does amazing things for those who lay aside everything displeasing to him, whose affections and obedience center on him.*

This is still a problem for Christians today. With all the temptations for things, prestige, success, reputation, approval, power, or any number of other idols, believers fall into the trap of developing great affection for the world. It is not that we do not have affection for Christ. Rather, in our affection for all the stuff and all the competing activities for our time, we tend to do those actions that bring us what we have the most affection for. Unfortunately, all too often it is not Christ. This goes for church leaders as well.

FACING THE OBSTACLE (OUR JORDAN)

It finally happened. Israel crossed over into the Promised Land. We can only imagine what it would have been like to witness such a large mass of people moving as one across the same place where not long before floodwaters were rushing by.

To provide Israel with a reminder of what God did the day he brought them across, Joshua erected stones into a memorial (Josh. 4). Joshua must have known how Israel tended to forget God's past mighty deeds.

Leaders, how many times in our churches have we witnessed God doing something significant, and have essentially forgotten it a year later? Perhaps there are some creative ways we can keep a memorial—a symbol that can remind our congregations of what God is doing.

Principle 4: *Memories of God's miracles grow dim with time. Memorials can help keep the memories in front of us.*

PREPARE TO DEFEAT YOUR JERICHO

Now on the west side of the Jordan, God told Joshua to do something that was risky militarily. Joshua had the people set up camp right on the eastern border of the Jericho area. Then he circumcised the men within striking distance from Jericho. During the time of the healing, the entire nation was vulnerable to an attack by Jericho or anyone else (Josh. 5:2–8). Why would God have them circumcised at this vulnerable place? Why would God not have had them do this surgery on the east side of the Jordan? Or why would God not have at least had them do the surgery in stages, a small percentage of the men at a time, and therefore provide for the protection of Israel? All I can infer is that God wanted the nation to see his hand of protection while they were most vulnerable and while they were being obedient.

Many churches make foolish decisions, stating that what they were doing was in obedience to God, when it was not. Churches build new, excessive buildings with enormous debt out of what they call "obedience," when instead, it was out of their affection for respect or recognition in the community. People set out into full-time Christian work, without any source of support, declaring that they are stepping out in obedience, when their real motivation is to leave another unpleasant situation.

On the other hand, I have known men and women who have genuinely stepped out in faith for God and have seen God provide in wonderful ways. I know missionaries who have selflessly stepped into impossible situations and been fully protected and provided for.

It can be difficult to discern between foolishness and obedience. We keep going back to the fundamentals: Scripture, prayer, godly counsel, looking for idols in our hearts, and examining our motivations. As Paul warns us, many times the flesh (our affection for power, respect, approval, recognition, or safety) can be what is motivating us. Paul warns us always to be on guard.

Principle 5: *Obedience to God is the best choice even if it appears foolish. Our Lord is the God of impossibilities and kept promises.*

The specific steps in the strategy that God had Israel take to defeat Jericho were incomprehensible. Think about it—march around the city a bunch of times, blow some horns, yell loudly, and the walls will come down. No way will it happen. It had never been done before. It flew in the face of military strategy. It was contrary to common sense. It defied the laws of natural science (Josh. 6:3–5). Yet it happened!

Principle 6: *Anything God intends to do, he will do, including keeping his promises.*

BUDGETING

In this book, we will not be going into all the details of quality budgeting. We will attempt to bring some sense of direction in order to make the connection with the overall plan.

The budget has four parts; the first three are estimates and the fourth is a report:

1. The cash income (sources of money from giving, the sale of assets, and new long-term debt)
2. The cash outgo (which includes ministry costs/expenses, purchase of capitalized assets, and the payments on debt)
3. The cash flow (the forecast of the money coming in and the money going out through the period of the budget)
4. The variance report (a report that compares, usually monthly, the actual cash income and cash outgo to the forecasted cash income and cash outgo, for the purpose of identifying areas of significant differences between the two)

The Budget has five goals:

1. To provide an estimate of the costs of the ministries included within the vision God has given your church, and to compare it against the anticipated cash income to assure that there is sufficient income to cover the cash outgo

2. To provide an estimate of the costs to compare against the actual costs for the purpose of the evaluation of the ministries
3. To provide for an estimated cash flow to assure that each month there will be adequate financial reserves to fund the monthly ministry cost inherent within the vision
4. To provide a basis for planning in future years
5. To provide information in a format that will allow for communication and discussion

Many churches fail to understand the importance of a comprehensive financial-management plan, including financial statements (balance sheet, income statement, and reconciliation of cash report) and a forecasted budget.

For most churches, which do not have a comprehensive financial-management plan, it will take years to get there. However, if you are one of those and you desire to have a quality plan, you can do it.

There is inexpensive software, there are books and seminars on church accounting and reporting, and there are advisors who can coach you. The first decision is to move in that direction. We have seen it done by people who had very little knowledge or experience in this field. Please, do not let fear hold you back. Take it one step at a time, and you will get there.

PENCIL PLANNING

After all this discussion about planning and budgeting, we must be careful never to let the plan become sovereign. Only God is sovereign. Therefore, do planning with a pencil. In other words, we must be ready to change direction as God directs us.

Even a seemingly secular subject like planning, as with all things, revolves around Christ. We must keep planning centered on God's purpose and mission as well as his vision for our church. Planning is important; but never forget that God loves people, not planning.

In the next chapter, we will be looking at organizing our team.

CHAPTER 14

ORGANIZING THE TEAM

A decade ago, I (Tim) walked into a second-story office for the Galesburg, Illinois, evangelistic festival with Dan Owens. Dan was not organizing the mass evangelism event, but was concerned that much needed to be accomplished to prepare for his forthcoming crusade. A local businessman had given the invitation for Dan to come. Even with a passion for the lost in his city, this dear business-man lacked the administrative gifts necessary to carry out the mission. He had a dream, but no skill to carry out the dream. It was comical to walk into such a situation and realize the only hope was for God to act.

There was no apparent organization or structure, so the Luis Palau Association contributed a very seasoned administrator to help. But frankly, it was God working through the faith of one man more than any of our team's abilities. Yes, the Spirit of God does move often in mysterious ways. However, routinely God works through the gifted people in his church.

Paul left Titus in Crete to "straighten out what was left unfinished and appoint elders in every town, as I directed you" (Titus 1:5). The exhortation implies that Titus had unfinished business to attend to—a work that Paul had started. Titus had to correct what was wrong and solve problems—basically, giving order and structure to a chaotic situation. He appointed men to continue maintaining the orderliness of church life. Paul taught the church in Corinth that God had given the gift of administration to some to strengthen the church in her need for order and direction. Paul's list of gifts to the church included leadership. God calls those who lead the church to do so with diligence (Rom. 12:8). The gift of leadership means that someone stands in front to point the way.

Structure is to the church what a skeleton is to the body. An emaciated body lacks muscle, making the skeleton blatantly obvious. An obese body camouflages any skeleton, while placing extreme pressure on the skeletal system. A healthy body shows the flesh and bone in balanced proportions. The church or Christian organization that has structure and organization in balance with vision and resources will experience effectiveness and efficiency. When the organization continues to debate roles, priorities, and regularly seeks to "reorganize," then the management process is out of balance.

Relational conflicts within the church often come because people are confused or frustrated. When leaders neglect organizational structure, the ministry environment feels unsafe and confusing. Overstructured ministries often restrict new people and new ideas from being welcomed. How can you know if the structure of your ministry or church is healthy? Look for the signs.

PROJECTS GET DONE

When people are properly organized, they become efficient and effective in accomplishing the tasks required of them. Properly structured churches find that people work together and accomplish given tasks with a sense of ease and harmony. The Luis Palau Association has a top-notch volunteer program. Dozens of volunteers give thousands of hours each year to assist the Palau Association in accomplishing a number of major ministries. One very time-consuming ministry is the direct-mail ministry. The volunteers prepare and send out thousands of mailings every year. What makes this a successful program? The volunteer coordinators do a great job of organizing people—they explain tasks clearly, make sure resources are readily available, provide refreshments, keep a well-lit and clean environment for the volunteers, and are contacted well in advance. Also, public recognition encourages them to keep up their commitment to the team.

PEOPLE ARE HIGHLY VALUED

When people feel appreciated, they will give the extra hour, drive the extra mile, and work in less-than-ideal situations. Ministry is not just about tasks, but about people who desire to be productive and appreciated for their efforts. When the system is in place to demonstrate value to people for their efforts, they will go out of their way to accomplish the tasks set before them. When people feel welcomed and wanted, the air is abuzz with conversations and people's faces have pleasant expressions. People are valued because the supervisors tell them so. They are rewarded with affirming words and public recognition for service and achievements. Service awards demonstrate that people are valued by the organization. Public acknowledgments for work well done, sacrifices made, and innovative ideas contribute to a team excelling in all they do.

When crisis comes to the individual team member, the reaction of the other team members demonstrates the value of the individual to the team. A dear friend just recently commented to me (Tim) that, when his wife faced a health crisis, the people where he worked extended much grace and support to him and his wife. Why? Because they highly value people and relationships. What did that bring to my friend? Safety and security in a time of great stress and pain. The institutional value—that people are important—brought strength and hope at a critical time. God's love needs arms to hug and shoulders to lean on. Do you highly value people?

PROBLEMS GET SOLVED

Proper organization promotes the solution of problems of all shapes and sizes. Healthy structures within the organization promote excellent communication and collaboration in problem solving. Organizations with ten members or ten thousand members are healthy when they can solve all types of problems. To have a healthy structure, you need clear and positive lines of communication. Nothing is more frustrating in an organizational environment than when you do not know whom to ask to give you an answer for your problem. However, when there are clear roles and responsibilities that outline who relates to whom, for what reasons, and with ample resources, then a healthy environment of grace promotes wholesome relationships and productive people.

Recently, I (Tim) was looking for an updated résumé of a leader in our organization. The department that formerly handled such matters no longer existed. What was handled under one department now existed under various departments. So one phone call led to another, some in the office, others across the nation. But, at the end of the day, no one knew who was responsible for what. Eventually my questions were answered and I got the résumé, but at the cost of far too many hours.

In contrast, when people know where to go and whom to ask in solving problems, both the individuals and the team within the organization excel.

COMMUNICATION IS OPEN AND CLEAR

By communication, we mean verbal and written, short and long term, in the office and on the road, in private and in public. Communication is to relationships what blood is to the body, says our friend Bobb Biehl. Without clear, regular, emotionally connected communication between all members of the team, confusion and conflict will flourish.

Healthy communication will promote relationships being built, problems being solved, and projects getting accomplished. With healthy communication, people are happier and healthier.

Poor communication causes a breakdown in relationships. When relationships deteriorate, people lose trust and become defensive. People become more prone to hiding their feelings, ideas, and contributions to solving problems. Eventually the covering up of feelings will explode in inappropriate outbursts of anger, bitterness, and accusations. Unhealthy words will cultivate feelings of resentment and bitterness. A cycle of guilt will promote critical attitudes, and a spirit of judgment will invade the organization.

However, when leaders welcome the communication of feelings and ideas, successes and failures, hopes and sorrows, people will flourish in their interpersonal relationships. The team will feel good about itself. People will express creativity and hope for the future. Everyone will do better. The team will be productive.

Leaders Have a Choice

Leaders have a unique role in formulating how the vision will be accomplished. Chapter 13 dealt with planning. Planning and structure (organization) require consistent interaction. You could develop structure before, at the same time as, or after planning. The important reality is that these two components of organizational leadership must work together.

One of the key steps in developing the plan is defining how your ministry will be structured in order to fulfill the vision. One of these first steps is to determine the five to seven areas on which the ministry will be focused. What are the major areas of ministry? What specific groupings will we create to build team ministries?

Typically, a church may divide the responsibilities along the lines of topic or age groups (life phases). For example, a church may have children's ministry, youth ministry, adult ministry, worship, missions, and administration. There could also be a structure that looks something like this: worship, outreach, education, missions, and administration. Obviously there are subgroupings under each major focus, but age groupings or topical groupings are the typical way of structuring ministry.

The parachurch or missions organization could adopt a geographical or topical approach to structure, depending on what the leadership decided was important. We recommend no more than five to seven major divisions (departments) in an organization.

Once we decide upon the basic format or structure, then we must ask a number of key questions. Let us consider a few of these key questions:

1. *Who is responsible for what?* Within each major division or department, individuals will take on specific roles and tasks. You need to clarify what you want each person to do. This defines what projects the person is to be participating in or leading. The "what" question addresses the actual tasks a person will be involved with.

2. *Who is responsible for whom?* This question addresses the team in terms of relationships. You must define who will be working with or supervising whom. The focus here is not on tasks, but on relationships. Therefore, the supervisor needs to address questions that deal with feelings, not just outcomes. What a person does is important, but more significantly for those in ministry, it raises the issue of *how* the person is doing. What is the person learning? How is the person growing?

3. *Do we have the right people in the right place at the right time with the right responsibilities?* A question of "fit" stands out to all of us as you look at the church as a body working together. There is nothing more frustrating than trying to replace a lost screw and realizing that the new one is the wrong size. As the saying goes, "You can't put a square peg in round hole." Leaders will often ask people to serve in specific ministries because of a great need. This may be okay for a short period of time, but for the long term, people flourish because their "fit for ministry complements their gifts, talents, and calling."[1]

TOOLS TO FACILITATE PEOPLE
IN ACCOMPLISHING THEIR TASKS

What tools would you need to answer the question "How will the ministry be structured?" First would be an organizational chart. This chart attempts to put into a graphic format the relationships and responsibilities of those serving in ministry. The most basic function of an organizational chart is to answer the question "What is the big picture?" How will the major areas of the ministry be organized? What focuses of ministry will we continue to work on for years to come?

The organizational chart can also answer the question "Who is responsible for what?" It puts into graphic format the personnel who will be involved. Along with the major focus of the ministry, the organizational chart will have names attached to each specific ministry.

Several factors can contribute to your understanding of the health of your organization. As you look at the organizational chart, ask yourself these questions:

1. Is any person responsible for more than five to seven areas?
2. Is any person directly supervising more than five to seven people?
3. Does any person report to more than one person?
4. Is each person relating to a team at his or her level of responsibility?

If you can answer yes to any of these questions, then you are heading for an unhealthy outcome.

Another tool for addressing the "who" question is having clear job descriptions for each person. This is applicable not only to paid positions, but also to volunteers working in the church. One church calls the form for the volunteers a *ministry focus sheet*. This allows the ministry leader to outline, discuss, and evaluate each person constructively.

Tools for Helping People in Their Relationships

Leaders facilitate healthy relationships when we become a student of people's personalities, spiritual gifts, relationship experiences, and ministry histories. Tools that help assess a person's personality style will enhance understanding of behaviors, reactions, relationships, and commitments to tasks and people. Role Preference, DISC, Meyers/Briggs, and TJTA are some of the tools that can assist in this analysis. Seeking to understand others before understanding self comes as a maxim from Stephen Covey.[2] The leader who applies this maxim through thoughtful and systematic application to the organization will find people far more eager to serve when they are understood for who they really are.

Tools, however, can never replace time spent in developing healthy and productive relationships. As Allen shared earlier, quality time comes only as a by-product of quantity of time. Therefore, to know and nurture healthy ministry relationships, teams must spend time together in a variety of contexts. Ministry only in the office setting limits one's knowledge and respect for others. Spending social time brings a greater level of appreciation for a person's wholeness.

I (Tim) loved working with our office administrator, Freda, some years ago at Palm Springs Baptist Church. She was multitalented and blessed with a passionate heart for God and people. But to see Freda in the context of her home was a real eye-opener. During my visit with her and her husband, I learned that not only was Freda skilled in relationships, but she was also very gifted as an artist, expressing herself in a multitude of creative crafts.

Freda's maturity and breadth of life experience brought real-life wisdom into our staff meetings. She understood practical things such as how long it would take to accomplish a specific task. She had the grace and wisdom to ask, "Pastor, can I involve some of the ladies in the church to help me send out the church newsletter?" This insight not only helped us complete a task on time, but it also gave meaningful ministry for a handful of older women who enjoyed the social side of their work.

A Radical Problem with Organization

In Latin, *radical* means "at the root."[3] At the root of much confusion in the life of the church lies the neglect of considering the working of the Holy Spirit in the administration of the church. This confusion and disorganization comes from several sources.

1. Those not gifted in administration attempt to administer the affairs of the church. This creates chaos. People become confused. Goals are not met. People tend to be in conflict. Focus of ministry runs in many directions. People are not managed well. Visionary leaders can become control freaks, not allowing others to participate in the management of great dreams and plans.
2. Some say that the church does not need to be organized. "Let the Spirit lead." Mostly what happens in those churches can be summarized in the phrase "We started well." But finishing a project, developing a ministry, growing to maturity are thoughts that fade quickly.
3. "Everything must be done decently and in order" hangs as an invisible banner over the front of some worship centers. The spirit of structure, process, and order can dominate the life of a congregation. Though people may feel safe in this environment, they most likely will become more like a machine than a community.

Those gifted by the Spirit with administrative gifts should be recognized and positioned to use their giftedness to serve the church. How can this be done?

1. Provide training in the local church for those with these gifts, through Bible schools and seminaries that educate people for such ministry. Often Christian schools do not prepare people with these gifts. Much of the pattern in the last decade or so is to recruit someone from the business world and place that person in the role as administrator of the church or Christian school. Yes, the Spirit gifts these people as administrators, but often they lack focused training for ministry within the church and Christian organizations.

2. Actively seek those with these gifts to serve in the church and Christian organizations. Challenge adult Christians with these gifts to consider leaving their secular positions for service in the church, Christian organizations, or missions organizations.
3. Place people with these gifts on boards of directors of churches and Christian organizations for the purpose of gaining from their insights, experience, and giftedness. Many churches and Christian ministries are dominated at the board level with people experienced and gifted in the area of teaching, pastoring, faith, etc., and therefore they lack the counsel of these seasoned and wise administrative persons.
4. Release these people to lead and manage the church. Often leaders don't allow these gifted people the freedom to really organize the church. Those gifted in the area of administration need the endorsement and affirmation of the pastor or board to be set free to manage as God has gifted them.

Allowing those gifted by the Spirit to organize and manage the church or parachurch organization can be tremendously freeing. Pastors and church boards need to identify and release people with these gifts. The church will find a healthier and happier experience of ministry when this happens.

Luis Palau is a dynamic, highly effective evangelist. Creative ideas and big visions never cease for Luis. On launching his own ministry in 1977, Luis saw a continual stream of employees come and go until he released the major administrative duties of the ministry over to David Jones, now CFO and VP of administration. David has the ability to filter and prioritize the vision. He understands process and clarifies roles and relationships. He recognizes the need for resources to accomplish the multitude of projects. All in all, the Holy Spirit has gifted David as an administrator in areas that Luis is not. When a team of individuals with unique gifts (of the Holy Spirit) came around Luis Palau, his ministry began to flourish. The Spirit of God works through people and structure to multiply ministries.

CHAPTER 15

SPIRIT-LED IMPLEMENTATION: FAITH IN ACTION

Throughout this book, we have challenged leaders to seek a continuously growing dependent love relationship with Jesus Christ, and from that relationship be his servant-leader in the life of your church and congregation. We have challenged you as a group to pray, to study, to share, to discuss, to discover, and to write out what you believe is God's purpose and mission. We have challenged you to discover God's vision for you—the clear, unique, and inspiring word picture of the ministry he intends for you and your church or your ministry for a time, which will be consistent with his purpose and mission.

We have challenged you servant-leaders to take on a balance of two roles: (1) to be Christ's steward, to lead Christ's people to carry out God's purpose and mission and his unique vision for your church or ministry, and (2) to be Christ's steward to serve, love, and develop those being led. It is within the context of all the previous chapters that we open the discussion on implementation.

IMPLEMENTATION IS "FAITH" IN ACTION

Suppose our congregation spent a year or two learning God's vision and plan for us to put new life into our congregation. We held meetings, surveyed the congregation for passions and gifting, surveyed the community for a profile of needs, and arrived at what we believed was God's unique vision for our congregation in this season of the life of our church. We carefully planned the detailed, measurable steps we would take to make God's vision a reality. We even worked out a budget to be sure we would be able to pay for the new thrust. We have put in thousands of hours of effort—but nothing happens. It takes faith to create a plan, but it takes *great faith* to implement a plan—that is where the risk is.

I (Allen) was meeting with a church in a situation similar to what we just described. They had done a lengthy analysis, held long sessions of prayer and discussion, and spent hours of writing to come up with a vision and plan. (They said they already had pur-pose and mission statements, which I did not see.) Since the church was in trouble at the time I was there, I asked them how it went when they implemented the plan they had put together. They answered that they never did get around to putting feet to the plan; it was in the filing cabinet gathering dust. Because they had never taken the first step, nothing changed that they had wanted to change.

Nothing ever happens with a vision and plan unless a leader directs the faith step. Joshua and Israel would have remained on the east side of the Jordan if Joshua had not led them to take the faith steps. Our church will have only a *dream* of new life if that faith step is never taken.

Taking those first and continuing faith steps is called *implementa-tion*. It is the process of making God's vision and plan for us a reality. Implementation is the "faith" ingredient in any intention to do some-thing differently. Read Hebrews 11 to see "faith" in action.

Unfortunately, implementing a plan (a change) is often poorly understood.

You may be asking, "What are you talking about? Making a plan happen cannot be all that difficult. It simply means to start taking the steps spelled out in the plan."

Achieving a quality Spirit-led and Spirit-driven implementation is a great deal more than just taking the first steps. It also involves dealing with the barriers we will encounter along the way.

PLANNING CHANGE

For years in banking, I (Allen) was involved in managing various changes and made many mistakes. Probably the most critical mistake I made was putting all my attention to coming up with an action plan to solve whatever problems we were dealing with. I had learned that problems were the difference between our current situation and what was desired. Therefore, all we needed to do was accurately decide what our current situation was, and what was ideal, and then arrive at a plan of action to make the change.

That approach worked for a while because no one was affected deeply. However, as we moved into the early 1990s and the banking industry entered what we called "merger mania," suddenly leadership was affecting lives deeply. People were losing or changing jobs and experiencing all the misgivings that come with job change.

Fortunately, the bank I was working for had a heart for the employees. Soon after a merger announcement came news of a transition plan—a plan to care for the staff whether they were being displaced or kept. What a revolutionary idea! Leaders had spent time coming up with a plan to care for us.

Admittedly, there was a business reason to explain a portion of the bank's care. The bank could not afford a mass exodus of the staff. And without some specific action, a mass exodus would have happened.

The bank, however, went much further than just preventing our mass exodus. In addition to an exit package for all displaced employees, regardless of position, it provided outplacement counseling, résumé-writing support, help in finding other jobs, and notice far in advance of the time management would displace people. The plan did not remove the fear reaction within the ranks, but it went a long way to reduce it, and I was introduced to a whole new world of managing change and transition. Christ used a secular organization to introduce me to what I now see is needed in many churches today—helping people deal with the fears that follow the change in their lives.

However, Christ was not through teaching me about transitioning people. Three years later, the next bank I was working for announced its merger, and once again I was back in the business of managing change and transition. Our Lord had more lessons for me to learn.

During this second merger and transition-management experience, I had the opportunity to become involved earlier. This chapter is largely what I learned from those two mergers and transitions—especially the second.

SPIRIT-LED IMPLEMENTATION

Please remember that you are a servant-leader, with two equally important roles—to be Christ's steward in the life of the church and his steward in the lives of those in the congregation.

We often think of implementation as a plan-oriented work. It is more than that. It is the work of discovering the purpose, mission, and vision as well. Even the activity of determining God's vision for our church will not happen if one or more leaders do not take the first step.

Coming up with God's purpose, mission, and unique vision statement for us does not just happen accidentally. It takes the right people (people who can set aside their personal agendas) and the best environment (where people are reasonably comfortable). It takes safe relationships (where people are acceptably comfortable with one another), organized and coordinated Scripture study, a focused prayer time, and a guarded discussion time where each person's safety is protected.

Intentional and careful work to discover God's vision is key to reaching a prayerfully thought-out purpose, mission, and vision statement.

One often forgotten factor in discovering God's vision for us is the time it requires. We cannot hurry this. We have heard of churches that have taken up to a year of prayer, study, and discussion to arrive at God's purpose and mission statement as well as their first well-prepared vision statement. There are likely other churches that may take as little time as one evening, although we doubt that one evening is enough time.

IMPLEMENTING THE WORK OF PLANNING

Planning is much like discovering vision; we will need the right people, the best environment, safe relationships, organized and coordinated Scripture study, a focused prayer time, and a guarded discussion time.

However, the planning process is more complicated. Purpose and mission are heavily theological. Vision is mixed. Some characteristics of vision are theological and some engage practical needs and problems.

Because planning deals with practical steps for practical needs and practical problems, it will engage a number of issues.

Evaluation of the Community

Since churches are located within communities and within neighborhoods, part of planning requires that leadership understand the nature of the people to whom they are called to minister. This will be information such as average age and family size, the number of single parents, varying ethnic backgrounds, population change, economic trends, and the political environment.

The community evaluation will include a look at unmet needs, such as poverty, youth problems, single-parent issues, young families, the elderly, hunger, and education.

Once we begin this type of analysis, we will find other subjects that will be helpful to know in order to build the church plan, especially God's plan.

An Internal Evaluation

The internal information about our own church that would be helpful to know and understand in planning could include, but is not limited to

- The profiles of those attending our church
- Exit interviews with those who have left the body
- Knowing the gifts, education, passions, and experiences of the members
- An understanding about the conflicts and sin within the congregation
- The saints consistently walking with Christ
- A capacity analysis of our facility (owned or rented)
- The leaders, current and potential
- The church capacities and passions available to meet the unmet needs of the community
- The amount of money available

God's Vision Statement Compared with God's Plan

As discussed in chapter 13, God's plan is God's vision statement expressed in measurable action steps. Discovering God's plan will require the same care and diligence that is needed to discover God's vision for us.

If part of God's vision for our church is a new evangelism thrust, God's plan will develop specific measurable steps to carry out that vision. The plan may include specific headings, such as "Develop a training program for evangelism" or "Create leadership for the program."

In the plan under the heading "Develop a training program," there will be specific actionable, measurable steps to take, such as "Choose five of the best evangelists from the congregation." Notice the step is measurable. We can tell when it starts and when it is completed. That is the key for all steps.

THE BUDGET

God's budget is God's action plan expressed in terms of money—the cost of doing the plan. Please refer to chapter 13 for a review of the budget. We do not intend to go into detail on developing the budget. Quality budgeting is a subject that would easily take an entire book to explain.

Your church will need people who are thorough, who do not take shortcuts. Your church will need people who can take the mountain of information, analyze it (keeping in mind God's purpose, mission, and vision), and put together a plan and budget to make it happen.

THE MAJOR BARRIER TO SPIRIT-LED IMPLEMENTATION
[BEFORE CONTINUING, IT MAY BE HELPFUL TO REVIEW CHAPTERS 6, 8, AND 9.]

In the "Valley of Difficult Leading" our leader has given us an assignment: to build a trail to a village in the mountains where the people are starving. While we will have many assistants from our "Valley of Difficult Leading" to help us, we will also have a number of opponents who will hinder us. But we are to love and protect them all, even the opponents whose intent is to stop or hurt us.

During the journey we are about to embark on, we will consistently meet our opponents, the "self-interest" and "fear" in other people. An opponent might even be another leader. Those opponents will be along the path, throwing things at us, trying to trip us, trying to confuse us by yelling or giving us false directions, and trying to frighten us into going back with false warning signs. They will be hiding from us (avoiding) or confronting us directly (attacking). But as challenging as those opponents will be, they will not be our most difficult problem.

Our most difficult problem will be the enemies of "self-interest" and "fear" within our own minds and hearts. Our enemies will tell us to look out for ourselves, to avoid our opponents, or if we cannot avoid them, to grab our swords and shields and defend ourselves. They will tell us that it is not our job to love and protect our opponents. If they cannot get on board, that is their problem. Our enemies within will tell us that we do not deserve this; it unfair for our leader to ask us to do this. If he knew our opponents like we do, he would not have asked us to love and protect them also.

This little story describes how it is when we are a servant-leader, being a steward for God, helping his people through the implementation of his plan. God is the leader who has asked us to implement his particular plan while loving and protecting even our opponents—his children who are against his plan. The enemy within us is real. That enemy is the flesh, which we have addressed throughout this book, and Paul revealed in the fifth chapter of his letter to the Galatians.

We could make it easy on ourselves if we backed off the scope of God's plan, which he asked us to implement with his leading. Remember that we are servant-leaders, with all that we now know it means. We have two roles and BOTH need our attention. It is a servant-leader's job to lead and manage the implementation of God's plan through the quagmire of opponents, while fighting off the enemies in our minds and hearts. The most challenging nature of this adventure is that our assignment from God is to get the church successfully through implementation while loving and protecting everyone, including all of our opponents. How likely is it that we will do a perfect job in our assignment? It is not likely, but it is our assignment.

How about that! And you thought that implementation was going to be a piece of cake.

PREPARATION

Here are five suggestions for leaders as we prepare for our roles in the Spirit-led implementation:

1. Remember our two new roles as a servant-leader: a) to be Christ's steward, to lead his people to carry out God's purpose and mission, and his vision for the church, and b) to be Christ's steward, to serve, love, and develop those being led.
2. Read chapter 9 again, focusing on ideas to help people with their fears.
3. Buy and read the book *Managing Transitions* by William Bridges. This book is a practical book covering the subject of helping to transition people, and covering it much more thoroughly than can be done in this short space.
4. Be sensitive to our own fears (reread chapter 8).
5. Talk to God constantly.

One of my favorite Scriptures on fear is what God said to Joshua as he handed Joshua the enormous job of leading his people into the Promised Land.

> Be strong and courageous, because you will lead these people to inherit the land I swore to their forefathers to give them. Be strong and very courageous. Be careful to obey all the law my servant Moses gave you; do not turn from it to the right or to the left, that you may be successful wherever you go. Do not let this Book of the Law depart from your mouth; meditate on it day and night, so that you may be careful to do everything written in it. Then you will be prosperous and successful. Have I not commanded you? Be strong and courageous. Do not be terrified; do not be discouraged, for the LORD your God will be with you wherever you go. (Josh. 1:6–9)

Christian leaders, I believe God is still telling us to be strong and courageous and careful to obey. God is telling us not to be terrified or discouraged; he is with us.

During the second bank merger discussed earlier in this chapter, we became aware that there was a sense of helplessness within the staff. Morale was lower than low. People were ready to give up, which would hurt both them and the merger process. We determined that it would be good if we could provide something that would cause forward thinking, something that would help people think optimistically about the future, and the president thought it was right and ethical to do something for the staff. We came up with training.

Why would you train people who are leaving? Where is the return in that? Contrary to what you might think, there was a return. For the company, it resulted in stronger participation in the merger process, and it was consistent with corporate values. Additionally, knowing that leadership did care helped the staff feel more valued. They began to think more optimistically about the next step in their lives. It was the right thing to do.

If developing people could help displaced bankers, what could it do for believers who are going through their transition and its resulting fear?

DEVELOPING PEOPLE AS PART OF AN IMPLEMENTATION STRATEGY

Developing people during the implementation of God's plan has two benefits: 1) it will help leaders, staff, and the congregation adopt *possibility thinking*, and 2) it will provide a source of quality new leaders for the time of growth we will experience because of the change.

Possibility Minded

Often during transition within an organization, including a church, people start thinking back to when everything was safe, back to the way it used to be. It is a normal reaction.

Training people, especially with a development plan designed uniquely for each individual, will help people start thinking about *possibilities*, including new ways that God may use them. It will help people begin to think of themselves differently, viewing themselves as part of God's vision for the church. Each person is a unique person in the church and needs to know it.

Leaders for the Future

In the future, our church will need new leaders, either to provide for the additional members in our congregation or to replace existing leaders who leave. The only way to avoid the need for new leaders is to close our church or let it die slowly.

However, if our church is growing, I cannot think of a better way to find our new leaders than growing them ourselves. It is amazing how few churches have a leadership-development plan. If we are one of those, implementing a development plan simultaneously with the implementation of God's new vision for our church will be a double blessing.

A leader-development ministry in our church is a renewal ministry, a morale-improvement ministry, a growth ministry, and a possibility-thinking ministry. A leader-development ministry is a ministry from which will flow future pastors, missionaries, Sunday-school directors, elders, deacons, worship leaders, and stronger families. A leader-development ministry will do a great deal to provide a strong leadership pool that will accept future leadership responsibilities.

So How Do We Carry Out Spirit-Led Implementation?

By now, we have God's purpose and mission, and we have God's unique vision for our church. We also now have a carefully selected team of leaders and a structure in which to lead. Our leaders have embraced their new roles as servant-leaders in addition to having skill in dealing with their own fears and the fears of other people.

There are four essentials for our church to take us into Spirit-led implementation:

1. Knowledge about and a passion for God's purpose and mission, as well as God's unique vision for our church
2. Leaders individually and as a group spending time with God in the Bible, in conversation with him (prayer) for the purpose of falling more in love with Jesus Christ, and allowing his love to flow through us into others
3. The willingness and skill to plan, budget, and implement whatever changes God may lead us to make
4. Servant-leaders with two roles: 1) to be Christ's steward, to lead his people to accomplish God's purpose and mission and his vision for the church, and 2) to be Christ's steward to serve, love, and develop those being led

THE NEEDED IMPLEMENTATION TEAM

To facilitate implementation, we will need leaders prepared for the role of implementation. We suggest three groups plus one individual.

1. The core senior leadership of our church should be the core servant-leaders. Their roles are to be
    *   High-level decision makers
    *   Role models of servant leadership (crucified self-interest and fear)
    *   The key instructors on servant leadership
    *   Attendees at church and group parties for the sole purpose of hearing the heart of the church and its congregation, using the key skills of asking questions and listening (not to interrogate people or to sell the plan)
    *   Free from defensive behavior when being verbally attacked
2. Ministry leaders with key roles in both directing ministry and facilitating change—to be thoroughly trained as servant-leaders with the tasks of
    *   Maintaining ministry quality
    *   Facilitating and supporting the planned changes in their ministry

- Loving and protecting all people in their ministry area, regardless of whether they are supporting the plan
- Remaining above defensive behavior when being verbally attacked

3. The minister and leadership development team:
   - The role of this position would be to facilitate discussion and agreement with the ministry heads regarding a development plan, given the interests, skills, and passions of individuals in the congregation desiring ministry or leadership development.
   - These individuals will need to be mature servant-leaders, able to walk the line between ministry need and leadership development.
   - These individuals will need to live above defensive behavior when verbally attacked.

4. One person in the temporary position of senior servant-leader:
   - This position is responsible for establishing a structure for accountability, tracking, and reporting.
   - This position is responsible for assuring that God's purpose and mission and God's unique vision for this church are being implemented according to the plan and budget.
   - This position is responsible for making sure that all leaders and members of the congregation are being loved and protected during the process of implementation.
   - This position will have to be strongly able to absorb the defensive behavior of people (attacking or avoiding), without reacting defensively in return, but instead loving and protecting them all.

IT IS ALL ABOUT GOD

We have not given you all you need to be skillful at planning and implementing. There are a number of excellent resources available to help you. Here is just a sample of what is available.

Bobb Biehl's book titled *Masterplanning* provides specific steps, a chart to aid you, and suggestions about procedures and much more.

Aubrey Malphurs' book *Advanced Strategic Planning* provides a comprehensive model for strategic planning.

We suggest that you look into some project software to help you organize and manage the intricacies of a plan: assigning resources, managing linkages, tracking progress, and fostering communication. If you do decide to use software to help you, we suggest that you give the task of managing the software to one or two people as support to the core servant-leaders.

It is not our goal to give you or direct you to a specific leadership form or model. It is our prayer that regardless of what form or model you choose to use, you will overlay the entire process with Christ's love and sovereignty over his church and the lives of his children and his call to you to come to him, to love him with all you are, to love others, and to go make disciples.

The church is not a service club or a business that can be led and managed only using skills and principles. The church is special in God's creation, and Christ is the head of the church. Christ is to lead your congregation, and you are his servant-leader.

CHAPTER 16

RENEWING PEOPLE AND MINISTRY

Elijah found that total dedication and service to the Lord came at great physical and mental costs. Having displayed extraordinary courage and power in the face of the prophets of Baal, Elijah saw the Lord's mighty power in consuming the sacrifices on Mount Carmel. Judgment came upon the false prophets, and vindication of the power of Yahweh was seen as never before.

Having been used of the Lord in such a powerful way, Elijah ran a marathon distance ahead of Ahab to Jezreel. You would think that such a strong act would melt the heart of any person, yet Jezebel's anger was expressed to Elijah in these words: "May the gods deal with me, be it ever so severely, if by this time tomorrow I do not make your life like that of one of them" (1 Kings 19:2).

According to the Scripture, Elijah was overcome with fear and he ran for his life. Possibly this was the smart thing to do. He ran the full length of Israel to Beersheba. Leaving his servant there, he continued into the desert. There, all alone under a broom tree, his true feelings gushed from his lips in these words: "I have had enough, LORD.... Take my life" (1 Kings 19:4). Elijah was exhausted, deeply depressed, and in great need of rest and renewal. Do you have a need for renewal?

God allowed him to sleep, eat, and hear his voice afresh. What a profound experience this was for Elijah. And it is a pattern for us.

Strengthened by food, drink, and rest, Elijah travel forty days to Mount Horeb where the Lord met him in a fresh, personal, and dramatic way. We all remember the story of the great and powerful wind, the earthquake, and then the fire, but no message from God. And then "after the fire came a gentle whisper" (1 Kings 19:12). Yes, with the whisper came a new dialogue with the Lord. Elijah expressed disappointment and doubt. God listened. God recommissioned him. Elijah obeyed.

We are all in need of rest and renewal—not just occasionally, but regularly. As individuals, families, churches, and Christian organizations, we need renewing. What we know and experience as individuals with God we need to experience as communities living for and serving God. Presented to us here is the need for renewal as a strategic part of managing our organization. Managing the people of God means that we prepare for renewal, not wait for some crisis to force the issue.

A number of expressions of this planned renewal come to mind. God orchestrated the calendar for the nation of Israel by including special times each year for worship and renewal (Lev. 23). During the 1980s, I (Tim) had the privilege to pastor Palm Springs Baptist Church. One of the special ministries for me during those years was developing our ministry to families. With the suggestion of an older pastor in our denomination, I began preaching a series of messages each year from Mother's Day to Father's Day relating to family issues. In addition, we began an annual retreat for couples. After a few years, one of the younger couples came to me an asked to begin leading this ministry because of the growth in their own lives from what we had been doing. Renewal loves to renew others.

THE BASIS FOR RENEWAL

Renewal flows from careful times of evaluation. When the management cycle comes full circle, sufficient information has been gained to say that some refinements need to be made. This is normal, healthy, and desirable. Renewal is based upon the need for change—personal change and corporate change. Leadership needs to model the need for change based upon seasons of personal evaluation and renewal.

What does the Bible say about evaluation? God is an evaluator. The apostle Peter said, "They [the pagans] will have to give account to him who is ready to judge the living and the dead" (1 Peter 4:5). Paul told the church in Corinth, "We [Christians] must all appear before the judgment seat of Christ" (2 Cor. 5:10). The Word of God is his instrument of evaluation, "for the word of God is living and active … it judges the thoughts and attitudes of the heart" (Heb. 4:12). The Father has delegated to the Son the responsibility of judgment, "and he [Father] has given him [the Son] authority to judge" (John 5:27).

As Christians, we are to evaluate ourselves. "Examine yourselves to see whether you are in the faith" (2 Cor. 13:5). Jesus taught, "First take the plank out of your own eye, and then you will see clearly to remove the speck from your brother's eye" (Matt. 7:5). Personal evaluation should precede and take precedence over the evaluation of others. Then we are called to evaluate others for leadership (Acts 6:1–3) and personal behavior (Col. 1:28; Matt. 18:15–18; Gal. 6:1). Lastly, we are to evaluate the world (Rom. 12:2; 1 John 4:1; 1 Thess. 5:21).

Evaluation of oneself and the ministry of the church or Christian organization should lead to praise for the blessings and fruitfulness of ministry. Praise for God and his family should be a first priority in evaluation. A Lord's Day psalm includes this note of praise: "but you have made me as strong as a wild bull. How refreshed I am by your power … the godly will flourish like palm trees…. Even in old age they will still produce fruit; they will remain vital and green" (Ps. 92:10–14 NLT).

Proper evaluation also leads to admitting the need for change. By regular and intentional self-examination, the Christian can stay close to Christ. Paul exhorts the believers in Rome to offer their bodies "as living sacrifices, holy and pleasing to God—this is your spiritual act of worship … be transformed by the renewing of your mind" (Rom. 12:1–2). This transformation of mind comes in view of God's mercy. The message to the Romans that precedes chapter 12 outlines the mercies of God. Here one finds the content for personal transformation.

In What Areas Should Renewal Take Place?

Psalm 78:72 (NLT) reflects God's evaluation of David the shepherd of Israel: "He cared for them with a true heart and led them with skillful hands." Renewal needs to touch our hearts and our hands, our inner lives and our leadership skills. Therefore, when thinking of renewing the church or Christian organization, we leaders need to begin with ourselves and then find pathways for every person in the organization to be touched regularly by the process of renewal. Rather than viewing renewal and retooling as an "emergency" measure, Spirit-led leaders intentionally make time for periods of evaluation and renewal.

The priority of heart over hand surprises no one. Leaders in the church understand that inner transformation and renewal pave the way in God's agenda for growth in leadership skills. Therefore, like David, we need to say, "Create in me a pure heart, O God, and renew a steadfast spirit within me" (Ps. 51:10). Or as he said in Psalm 139:23–24 (NLT), "Search me, O God, and know my heart; test me and know my thoughts. Point out anything in me that offends you, and lead me along the path of everlasting life." Or as John the beloved apostle exhorted the churches of Turkey, "Anyone who is willing to hear should listen to the Spirit and understand what the Spirit is saying to the churches" (Rev. 3:6 NLT).

In addition, as leaders of a church or Christian organization, we must develop our skills in ministry. These skills cover the breadth of what God has asked each of us to accomplish in our particular culture and ministry setting. We trust, for example, that this book will give you insights for integrating the working of the Holy Spirit in and through you in terms of leadership and management processes.

Leadership and management skills must be learned and refined. We each have our area of ministry that requires continued growth. With the abundance of information and resources available to grow in leadership skills, communication skills, interpersonal-relationship skills, worship and music skills, fund-raising skills, etc., we have many choices on how we want to integrate the additional knowledge and skills. We do not want to assume we know it all. We often forget more than we want to admit. The Holy Spirit maximizes what he wants to accomplish through our skills. The discipline to learn and master new skills challenges each of us in our service for the Lord.

I (Tim) never imaged that obtaining a Doctor of Ministry degree from Fuller Seminary in 1994 would be used for the Lord to open a door of ministry for me at Multnomah Biblical Seminary in 1996. I had hoped that someday in the distant future I might teach at a Bible college or seminary. Because I had a doctorate degree, God used me at an unexpected time to teach at the Multnomah seminary. For me, doctoral level studies not only prepared me for more effective ministry, but also opened a door for teaching at a graduate level.

So we have need for heart and hand renewal. As we gain skill in ministry, it should never be separated from our need for the renewal of our hearts. For personal renewal cannot be disconnected from the practice of corporate renewal. When the church participates in the Lord's Supper, Paul says we are to examine ourselves and make things right with other believers before partaking of the bread and the cup (1 Cor. 11:23–24). The church needs renewal in its ministries just as urgently as the individual does.

How Can Renewal Be Implemented?

First, the elders of the church can lead by practicing renewal in their personal lives and at leadership meetings. Through worship, reflection, and prayer, the leaders should come before the Lord to seek his guidance in personal and corporate change. This can be done at the weekly or monthly meetings, before the congregation in times of worship, and on special occasions for retreats.

Second, the staff of the church should practice renewal in their staff meetings, as they lead various ministries in the church, and in special retreat settings. Since the staff evaluates on a more systematic basis, they need to lend their experience to empower others in this discipline. Unless we view evaluation as listening to the Lord and the needs of the community in order to refine and adjust how we are doing ministry, it becomes a meaningless exercise. The context of evaluation must be seeking to understand the working of the Holy Spirit in and through our lives. Renewal should be the goal of this process.

Third, the leaders and staff of the church should lead the congregation in seasons of renewal, emphasizing the working of God that leads us to praise him and seek his instruction on what we should stop doing, what we should start doing, and how we can do ministry better. In the process, people should be encouraged, exhorted, and appreciated. The goal of leadership in equipping the body of Christ is to build up the body of Christ, not tear it down. We are to seek the working of the body of Christ in unity and diversity. This takes clear leadership through the evaluation process, leading to times of renewal and refreshment (Eph. 4:12–32).

AN EXAMPLE OF RENEWAL IN THE MIDST OF MINISTRY

A godly statesman by the name of Nehemiah highlights the strategic role of renewal. Nehemiah captures the essence of leading and managing a group of people who were completely outside the plan of God. God first touched the heart of the leader, Nehemiah. Visiting the destroyed capital of Israel, Nehemiah saw firsthand the terrible and tragic condition of the city of his people. God put Nehemiah on his knees and planted a dream within his heart. Rising from the dust of Jerusalem in 445 BC, Nehemiah was a changed man. The burden for rebuilding Jerusalem grew within his heart as a fire kindled with dry timber and a strong wind.

The power of this story is magnified as we realize Ezra had rebuilt the temple some years before. Yet God was not satisfied with a shrine for the purposes of bringing sacrifices only. He wanted to see a fully functioning city with all the dynamics of family life, commerce, and government running at full speed. Why else rebuild the city walls? The city walls were the residence for many city dwellers, and the city gates were the places of commerce and government. I believe God wanted his glory seen in every aspect of life, and so did Nehemiah.

Prayer had ignited in Nehemiah a new boldness and resolve to restore what had been destroyed (Neh. 1:4). With a plan planted in his heart, he found God opening the heart of the king to finance the vision. With papers of empowerment, a blueprint in his mind, and a team to work with him, Nehemiah began the building. He delegated responsibilities to each clan according to their ancestral heritage. The people were highly invested before they moved the first rock. When opposition came, Nehemiah exercised wisdom and resolve. He renewed the oppressed workers with the challenge to have a trowel in one hand and a sword in the other. Renewal of spirit came with a challenge to face the schemes of the enemy with creativity and determination.

It took only fifty-two days to move thousands of rocks and construct hundreds of feet of the city wall (a casemate wall), all in the midst of verbal abuse and threats of all kinds. Amazing! Unbelievable! When people are renewed in heart and mind, mighty things can happen. But the project was not over until all shared in the celebration. Nehemiah understood that finishing the wall was not the ultimate goal—it was worshipping God in a renewed city! God wanted his people to enjoy the safety of the city and experience his presence in their midst. Nehemiah realized that renewal of their hearts would lead to worshipping God. And the worship of God would be not only a blessing to the few Jews then living in Jerusalem, but "the sound of rejoicing in Jerusalem could be heard far away" (Neh. 12:43). When God's people are renewed, the whole city will hear praises to God.

What Does Renewal Mean for the Church Today?

Renewal means that the church will be a healthy community where God is worshipped, believers are being transformed, and the community at large feels the presence of God.

Renewal means that the church is a happy and holy place. The worship of God will find center stage in the priorities of the church. Personal and corporate worship will dominate people's discussions and mediations. The awareness of a holy and loving God will fascinate the worshippers. Praise will characterize the times of worship. Somber people will take off their coats of depression and put on robes of joy. Renewal by the Holy Spirit will lift hearts above the burdens of the day.

The church will grow in holiness. When God is center stage, the focus is upon him, not us. When we look at him, his truth shines on us. We begin to see the darkness of our souls. The hidden sins become more public. Our hunger for purity and righteousness calls out to our own hearts to be more like him. When renewal comes, God's people turn toward the Lord with a new desire to be conformed to his image.

This means that as we lead and manage the church, we need to be asking questions like "Is God renewing our hearts and minds?" "Is there a hunger for God?" "Why?" "Why not?" Leadership and management for the purpose of efficiency without hunger for God is an exercise in carnality. We are called to consider the ways of God that lead us closer to him, not just make us a better organization. Therefore, the goal of the organization is to draw people closer to him.

Organizational management and leadership, like the skeletal structure of our bodies, are to "be there, but not be seen." As was said earlier, a starving or obese body is not healthy or efficient. But a body that is healthy needs a strong skeletal structure. Organizational leadership and management is that skeleton. When the Holy Spirit empowers those gifted to lead and manage the affairs of the church, they in turn submit to his leadership as servant-leaders, and with the church regularly seek the Lord through a skillful process of organizational leadership and management.

We long for renewal in our own lives. When we find that in his presence, his people find fullness of joy. Join us in renewing our passion for him and our commitment to be servants for Jesus' sake to the church he died for and now lives for.

A Pathway for the Leading of God's Spirit

We cannot emphasize enough that discovering God's purpose, mission, and vision for our churches needs to become a process, not just a one-time event. Leaders must embrace the management process, not just the process steps. Also, the process is one that needs constant prayer and listening to God. Points of change come consistently as we listen to the Spirit of Christ in asking key questions. Please refer to the chart cited in the readers' guide for the list of key questions. We will use these questions repeatedly as we move through the management cycle and as we review and renew the ministry plan. These key questions can also be used in problem solving to identify problems and their sources.

Hopefully, the following diagram will help us visualize the "big picture" of Spirit-led management. However, the most important step toward becoming a Spirit-driven church is being open to the Spirit's leading in both our personal life and the life of the church. Books, diagrams, and the greatest minds in the world are worthless if we do not invite God to take our churches and its leadership and guide us into his vision for us.

READERS' GUIDE

The questions below are provided to help you process and apply the material in each chapter. We encourage the leadership team to discuss and dialogue together using these questions as a guide.

CHAPTER 1
FROM DEATH TO LIFE

1. Reverend Hagelganz said, "We advised the brothers, above all things, keep in mind the Lord and handle everything in love." How might that advice be applicable today?

2. What do you think were the major difficulties within Central Evangelical?

3. What might a Christian have affection for that could be greater than his or her affection for Jesus Christ?

4. What might be evidence of a believer holding something or someone with greater affection than his or her affection for Christ?

CHAPTER 2
THE PULL OF CONFLICTING AFFECTIONS

1. Ezekiel 14 addresses idols and stumbling blocks. What might be idols and stumbling blocks for Christian leaders today?

2. For what are you dependent on Jesus Christ? For what are you NOT dependent on Jesus Christ?

3. Against what temptations or sins do you feel that Christian leaders need to be the most on guard?

CHAPTER 3
DISCOVERING A LOVING AND TRANSFORMING GOD

1. In what ways do you and other leaders intentionally spend time together to pray and study Scripture for the purpose of knowing Christ more and loving him more deeply?

2. What is of greater concern to you and the other leaders in your church: (a) the love for God of the leaders and members of your congregation, or (b) their Christian behavior? Why? What evidence in Scripture is there for your answer?

3. What evidence of the fruit of the Spirit do you find in your church?

4. What symptoms of the flesh do you observe within your church?

CHAPTER 4
SPIRITUAL LEADERSHIP

1. Describe in your own words the person that God desires to lead his church.

2. What three questions would you ask someone being interviewed for a leadership role in your church?

3. What is the difference between being filled with the Holy Spirit and being a mature, godly leader?

CHAPTER 5
HEARING GOD

1. Describe in your own words how a Christian hears from God.

2. What barriers would you suggest keep believers from knowing God's will?

3. Describe the competing noises for church leaders today.

4. If you spend hours a day in prayer and Bible study, how will that help God love you more?

5. If you spend more time each day pursuing Christ in prayer and Bible study, how might that affect your love for him?

CHAPTER 6
LOVING PEOPLE, NOT USING PEOPLE

1. Describe in your own words how church leaders can use people.

2. What is stewardship?

3. What does it mean for a leader to be Christ's steward to lead his people?

4. What does it mean for a leader to be Christ's steward to serve, love, and develop people?

CHAPTER 7
WHEN GOD SAYS NO

1. What noes do you hear from God at this point of your ministry?

2. How has God directed you by preventing certain ministries in your past?

3. In your current journey, answer these three questions:
   a. If not here, where? (New places)

   b. If not now, when? (Timing issue)

   c. If not in this way, how? (New methods)

CHAPTER 8
A GOOD KIND OF FEAR

1. What are the faces of fear in your life?

2. How are you responding to the fears in your life?

3. How will you apply the five steps to fearing the Lord to your own personal fears listed in the questions above?

CHAPTER 9
HELPING OTHERS DEAL WITH FEAR

1. Describe in your own words a time in your church when leadership attempted to make a change they viewed as positive, but there was a strong opposing reaction to the change from a number of the members.

2. Describe in your own words what strategies the "attackers" used to fight against or slow down the attempted change.

3. Did any leader notice any avoiders within the church? Did anyone quietly leave during or soon after the change? If anyone did notice the avoiders' struggle, what specifically brought it to leadership's attention?

4. Describe in your own words how leadership handled the anger and avoidance problem within the congregation.

CHAPTER 10
MAKING TOUGH DECISIONS

1. What hard decisions are you facing today? Write them down.

2. What factors make this decision a tough decision for you?

3. In processing your answer, ask and answer these questions:
   a. What Scriptures give insight to this decision?

   b. How have you prayed concerning this decision?

   c. Are you obeying God or trying to please people?

   d. What are the costs for or against this decision?

e.   Are you being completely honest in making this decision?

f.   What counsel have you received from others?

g.   Is this a decision you have to make?

h.   Will truth prevail in making your decision? How?

i.   Are your emotions allowing you to be a person of integrity?

CHAPTER 11
A PATHWAY FOR THE HOLY SPIRIT'S LEADERSHIP

1. Is there any known sin in your life or the life of your church? Confess it (1 John 1:9; Matt. 18:15–18)!

2. Submit your mind, emotions, and will to the Holy Spirit (Eph. 5:18–20).

3. Submit your words and behaviors to one another (Eph. 5:21).

4. What is your faith-size action plan?

5. Promise God you will live by faith in the leading of his Holy Spirit (Heb. 11:6).

CHAPTER 12
WHAT GOD HAS IN MIND

1. What is God's Jericho for your church?

2. What, if anything, is keeping you or your church from attempting your Jericho?

3. Use the following chart to enter your response for your church's purpose, mission, and unique vision.[1]

Process Step and Tools	Key Question(s)	Your Response
Purpose Life Focus sheet	Why do I exist? Why do we exist?	
Mission What biblical texts summarize our mission? What stories capture the essence of our mission?	What is the enduring biblical statement to which God is calling his church? What does God's Word say about our mission? Our church's mission? Our core values?	
Vision Brainstorm ideas What word pictures capture the passion of our vision?	What is the clear, unique, and inspiring word picture of the ministry God intends for us for a period of time, which will be consistent with his purpose and mission? What has God called us to do? What is our philosophy? How will we do ministry?	
Prayer and Planning		
Structure/Organization		
Implementation and Reporting		
Evaluation and Renewal		

CHAPTER 13
PLANNING

1. In what ways does next year's plan for your church show a dependence on God?

2. Describe some miracles that God has done within your church over the last several years.

3. What is the plan to defeat your Jericho?

4. Add another line to the chart by entering your response for your church's plan to accomplish God's unique vision for your church.[2]

PROCESS STEP AND TOOLS	KEY QUESTION(S)	OUR RESPONSE
PURPOSE		
MISSION		
VISION		
PRAYER AND PLANNING Write down and track goals and steps to achieving goals Budget and fund-raising Prayer list accompanying goals	What are the specific measurable steps needed near term to accomplish his vision within the context of God's purpose and mission through and in us? Who is responsible for what? What tasks are to be done? When are tasks to be done? What are the links between tasks? What are the specific goals? What are the specific steps to reach the goals? What is our action plan? What resources are needed to reach the goals?	
STRUCTURE/ORGANIZATION		
IMPLEMENTATION AND REPORTING		
EVALUATION AND RENEWAL		

CHAPTER 14
ORGANIZING THE TEAM

1. Would you say that your church is a healthy organization according to the four characteristics of a healthy organization described in this chapter? Why? Why not?

2. Who are those with the gift of administration in your church or Christian organization? What are they doing in ministry? Are they being equipped? How are they being affirmed?

3. Add another line to the chart by entering your response for your church's structure to accomplish God's plan for your church.[3]

PROCESS STEP AND TOOLS	KEY QUESTION(S)	OUR RESPONSE
PURPOSE		
MISSION		
VISION		
PRAYER AND PLANNING		
STRUCTURE/ORGANIZATION Develop org. chart Write job descriptions Spiritual gifts inventory	In what major areas do we need to divide the workload to keep the tasks manageable? Who is responsible for what? Who reports to whom? Who and where is the team?	
IMPLEMENTATION AND REPORTING		
EVALUATION AND RENEWAL		

CHAPTER 15
SPIRIT-LED IMPLEMENTATION: FAITH IN ACTION

1. In what ways is implementation a faith activity?

2. What difficulties has your church leadership had in implementing change in your church?

3. How are you as leaders helping people make the transition during implementation of change in your church?

4. Add another line to the chart by entering your response for your church's implementation strategy.[4]

PROCESS STEP AND TOOLS	KEY QUESTION(S)	OUR RESPONSE
PURPOSE		
MISSION		
VISION		
PRAYER AND PLANNING		
STRUCTURE/ORGANIZATION		
IMPLEMENTATION AND REPORTING Structure of team Timeline Reporting forms	Is there a strategy to implement the plan? Is there a strategy to transition the people with love? Who is responsible for what? When are tasks to be done?	
EVALUATION AND RENEWAL		

CHAPTER 16
RENEWING PEOPLE AND MINISTRY

1. Are you in need of renewal? How do you know? What indicators can you list that point to the need for personal renewal?

2. Is renewal a regular and planned part of your leadership process? Why? Why not? What steps can you take to implement renewal as a regular part of your leadership process?

3. Complete the chart by entering your response for your church's evaluation and renewal strategy.[5]

PROCESS STEP AND TOOLS	KEY QUESTION(S)	OUR RESPONSE
PURPOSE		
MISSION		
VISION		
PRAYER AND PLANNING		
STRUCTURE/ORGANIZATION		
IMPLEMENTATION AND REPORTING		
EVALUATION AND RENEWAL Reporting forms Job evaluation forms Refinement of goals Appreciation certificates Job descriptions refined Renew purpose and mission and refine the vision	Who will evaluate what? When will evaluations be done? What specific steps do we need to take to accomplish goals, refine goals, and refocus personnel?	

ABOUT THE AUTHORS

DR. TIMOTHY ROBNETT

Inspiring and equipping people for effective evangelism and church life is the focus of Tim's ministry.

Following his university training at Stanford, where Tim played football on two Rose Bowl championship teams, he interned as a youth minister at Peninsula Bible Church, where God sparked his desire for vocational ministry. After attending Western Seminary, he served as an associate pastor in Bakersfield and then as senior pastor of Palm Springs Baptist Church (Palm Springs, California) for eleven years. In 1994, Tim received his Doctor of Ministry degree from Fuller Theological Seminary in Pasadena, California.

Throughout his ministry, Tim has also given leadership to the Fellowship of Christian Athletes, Youth for Christ, and the Conservative Baptist Association of Southern California, and currently for the Proclamation Evangelism Network of Mission America.

Since 1990, Tim has served with the Luis Palau Association. His ministry has included directing international festivals in twelve nations, overseeing conferences and evangelist training sessions in many other nations, coordinating collaborative missions in several states in India and several African nations, and since 2000, directing the Next Generation Alliance ministry in equipping a new generation of proclamation evangelists.

Tim also served as an associate professor of Pastoral Ministry and Internship Director at Multnomah Biblical Seminary from 1996–2004. He coordinated the Master of Arts program in pastoral studies. He also developed additional majors in ministry management, evangelism, and family ministries.

Tim married his high-school sweetheart, Sharon, in 1971. They have two adult children, their son, Joel, and his wife, Kate, and their daughter, Karen. He enjoys horseback riding, weightlifting, racquetball, and gardening.

Allen H. Quist

Dr. Don Brake, dean and vice president of Multnomah Biblical Seminary, says, "Few men are more passionate and articulate about godly, biblical church management and leadership than Allen Quist."

This passion has developed from many years of experiences, beginning when Allen was a young boy. He first learned leadership from his father, who challenged him never to be a quitter. With this strong foundation, Allen went on to attend Washington State University, marry his college sweetheart, and begin a family and a thirty-five-year career in banking.

Besides graduating from Pacific Coast Banking School and Northwest Agricultural Credit School, Allen spent much of his last two decades in banking developing valuable leadership skills through managing small-business lending activities, leading a region of twenty-four retail branches, and helping manage change and transition up to and through two bank mergers.

During the later years of his banking career, Allen began participating in foreign missions and ministry-related activities. In 1998, feeling called to focus on his growing hunger to know Jesus Christ more deeply, Allen left his banking career to complete a Master of Arts in Pastoral Studies in 2002 at Multnomah Biblical Seminary.

Allen is now an adjunct faculty member at Multnomah Biblical Seminary in Portland, Oregon, and is currently enrolled at Regent University, working on a Doctorate in Strategic Leadership.

Along with Rick Battershell, CPA, and Troy Anderson, an attorney, Allen cofounded Ministry Management Seminars, a nonprofit organization dedicated to equipping church leaders on matters of accounting, law, financial management, strategic planning, conflict mediation, leadership refocusing, and church rebirthing.

Allen helps church leaders intentionally adopt a leadership model dependent on God's leading. As opportunities open, he shares his passion for leadership in other countries.

Allen and Mary reside in Troutdale, Oregon, near their two sons and daughter and their families.

To find out more about *The Spirit-Driven Church*,
download bonus material, or contact the authors, go to
spiritdrivenchurch.net.

NOTES

INTRODUCTION

1. Win Arn, *The Pastor's Manual for Effective Ministry* (Monrovia, CA: Church Growth, 1988), 16.

CHAPTER 1
FROM DEATH TO LIFE

1. Peter Drucker, *Managing the NonProfit Organization: Principles and Practices* (New York: HarperCollins, 1992), 113.
2. Arn, *The Pastor's Manual for Effective Ministry*, 16.
3. George Barna, *User Friendly Church* (Ventura, CA: Regal Books, 1991), 76.
4. Ibid.
5. William Bridges, *Managing Transitions* (Reading, MA: Perseus Books, 1991), 4.

CHAPTER 2
THE PULL OF CONFLICTING AFFECTIONS

1. Spiros Zodhiates, *The Complete Word Study Dictionary, New Testament* (Chattanooga, TN: AMG Publishers, 1993), 1280.
2. Henry Blackaby, *What the Spirit Is Saying to the Churches* (Sisters, OR: Multnomah Publishers, 2003), 37.

CHAPTER 3
DISCOVERING A LOVING AND TRANSFORMING GOD

1. Oswald Chambers, *My Utmost for His Highest* (Grand Rapids: Discovery House Publishers, 1992), March 12.

CHAPTER 5
HEARING GOD

1. David Bryant, *Christ Is All: A Joyful Manifesto on the Supremacy of God's Son* (New Providence, NJ: New Providence Publishers, 2004), 10–11.

CHAPTER 7
WHEN GOD SAYS NO

1. Luis Palau promotional video for the Portland Festival 2000.

CHAPTER 11
A PATHWAY FOR THE HOLY SPIRIT'S LEADERSHIP

1. Christian A. Schwarz, *Natural Church Development* (Carol Stream, IL: Churchsmart Resources, 1996), 28.
2. The Barna Group, "Small Churches Struggle to Grow Because of the People They Attract," *The Barna Update* (September 2, 2003), www.barna.org. Accessed July 25, 2005.
3. Bobb Biehl, *Masterplanning: A Complete Guide for Building a Strategic Plan for Your Business, Church, or Organization* (Nashville: Broadman & Holman, 1997); and Aubrey Malphurs, *Vision America: A Strategy for Reaching a Nation* (Grand Rapids: Baker Books, 1994).

CHAPTER 12
WHAT GOD HAS IN MIND

1. Aubrey Malphurs, *Advanced Strategic Planning* (Grand Rapids: Baker Books, 1999), 104–5.
2. Biehl, *Masterplanning*, 33.

3. Jan Johnson, *When the Soul Listens* (Colorado Springs: NavPress, 1999), 106.
4. Biehl, *Masterplanning*; and Malphurs, *Vision America*.

CHAPTER 14
ORGANIZING THE TEAM

1. Biehl, *Masterplanning*, 98–104.
2. Stephen Covey, *The 7 Habits of Highly Effective People* (New York: Simon & Schuster, 1989).
3. Webster's Seventh Collegiate Dictionary, s.v. "radical."

READERS' GUIDE

1. Biehl, *Masterplanning*; and Malphurs, *Vision America*.
2. Ibid.
3. Ibid.
4. Ibid.
5. Ibid.

Recommended Reading

Anderson, Neil T., and Charles Mylander. *Setting Your Church Free.* Ventura, CA: Regal Books, 1994.
    This book addresses the fundamental issues of church leadership today.

Biehl, Bobb. *Masterplanning: A Complete Guide for Building a Strategic Plan for Your Business, Church, or Organization.* Nashville: Broadman & Holman, 1997.
    Using a step-by-step process for leading an organization that begins with understanding and developing a heart-inspired vision, Biehl shows readers how they can turn that vision into reality for the church or mission's organization.

Bridges, William. *Managing Transitions.* Reading, MA: Perseus Books, 1991.
    William Bridges is both artful and accurate in his dealing with change and transition. This is an extremely useful work for churches that struggle with change because they fail to recognize the issue of fear that Bridges describes.

Clinton, J. Robert. *The Making of a Leader.* Colorado Springs: NavPress, 1988.
    Clinton offers a well-organized presentation of the stages of leadership growth and development.

Covey, Stephen R. *The 7 Habits of Highly Effective People.* New York: Simon & Schuster, 1989.
    Before you can lead others, you must order your personal life. Integrity demands congruity of heart and life. Covey shares effective

principles for achieving personal victory and then public victory, creating harmony in one's personal and public life.

Curtis, B., and J. Eldredge. *The Sacred Romance.* Nashville: Thomas Nelson Publishers, 1997.
 This is a wake-up book. While it is addressed to individuals, it takes little imagination to apply corporately. God is a lover, pursuing us into a loving and adventurous relationship with him.

George, Carl F., and Robert E. Logan. *Leading and Managing Your Church.* Grand Rapids: Fleming H. Revell, 1987.
 George and Logan present a unique approach to the everyday details of managing the church, seen through the eyes of one who equips God's people to do the work of ministry. This book includes many helpful principles for leading the people of God by the power of his Word and Spirit.

Malphurs, Aubrey. *Advanced Strategic Planning.* Grand Rapids: Baker Books, 1999.
 This book is rich with helpful ideas, presenting them in the context of a strategic-management model. This would be a good book for a management team such as a board of elders to work through together.

———. *Developing Vision for Ministry in the 21st Century.* Grand Rapids: Baker Books, 1992.
 This book lays out a step-by-step approach to creating a vision for your organization, with ample illustrations and worksheets to assist you in creating and implementing the vision.

———. *Doing Church: A Biblical Guide for Leading Ministries Through Change.* Grand Rapids: Kregel Publications, 1999.
 Don't let the size of the book fool you. It is a small book but it is thick with thought-provoking material.

———. *Values-Driven Leadership.* Grand Rapids: Baker Books, 1996.
 Malphurs presents an excellent and extensive survey in understanding the importance of discovering, clarifying, and using core values in leadership and organizational management.

———. *Vision America.* Grand Rapids: Baker Books, 1994.

Maxwell, John C. *The 21 Irrefutable Laws of Leadership.* Nashville: Thomas Nelson Publishers, 1998.
 Dynamic and practical, this book includes twenty-one principles that apply across the board for any leader and any leadership role.

Oncken III, William. *Monkey Business*. Provo, UT: Executive Excellence
    Publishing, 2000.
    This is a book on the art of delegation that you will never forget.

Sanders, J. Oswald. *Spiritual Leadership*. Chicago: Moody Press, 1977.
    Sanders focuses on the character qualities essential for a truly Spirit-
    filled and directed leader.

Schwarz, Christian A. *Natural Church Development*. Carol Stream, IL:
    ChurchSmart Resources, 1996.
    This book outlines basic principles and factors that contribute to
    church health and growth.

Stanley, Andrew. *Visioneering*. Sisters, OR: Multnomah Publishers, 1999.
    Through a study of the life of Nehemiah, Stanley applies age-old
    principles of leadership to leaders today in their challenge to create a
    biblical vision for ministry.

Westing, Harold J. *Church Staff Handbook*. Grand Rapids: Kregel
    Publications, 1997.
    A seasoned church leader shares practical insights for leading the
    church staff. Gives practical information on understanding leadership
    styles and team building, and demonstrates how the Spirit of God can
    engage in administrative processes.

Wilkes, C. Gene. *Jesus on Leadership*. Wheaton, IL: Tyndale House Publishers,
    1998.
    Wilkes makes a valuable contribution to understanding the unique
    qualities in Jesus as a leader. Practical descriptions and definitions of ser-
    vant leadership and how it works in today's world.